THE HOW TO BOOK
ON DIVIDEND GROWTH
INVESTING

THE HOW TO BOOK ON DIVIDEND GROWTH INVESTING

Create Generational Wealth and Passive Income for Life!

For information about this title or to order other books and/or electronic media, contact the publisher:

ACG Press
222 Lilly Rd. NE, Olympia, WA 98506
DoctorAce.com

ISBNs:
978-0-9753339-8-3 (softcover)
978-0-9753339-9-0 (eBook)

Printed in the United States of America

Cover and Interior design: 1106 Design

Table of Contents

Go to www.doctorace.com/dividendlinks/ to quickly access links to all the online resources that are referenced in this book.

About the Author

Dr. Albert "Ace" Goerig graduated from Case Western Reserve University Dental School in 1971 and was their distinguished alumnus in 2014. Following graduation, he joined the U.S. Army and retired as a colonel in 1991 after 20 years of distinguished military service.

In 2004, he wrote his first book: *Time and Money: Your Guide to Personal and Financial Freedom*. His most recent bestseller book, *The New Wealth Paradigm for Financial Freedom*, was published in May 2021 and is available on Amazon. He has a free website, www.doctorace.com, with audios and videos to help individuals quickly become debt-free and understand dividend investing.

Disclaimer

This guide is for informational and educational purposes only, based on the personal experience and research of the author. Information has been obtained from data sources considered to be reliable, but its accuracy and completeness are not guaranteed. This guide is offered with the understanding that the author and publisher are neither fiduciaries nor engaged in rendering legal, tax, investment, financial, or other advice. All content is general in nature, and your unique circumstances may include factors not considered by the author.

You assume sole responsibility for evaluating the merits and risks of the provided content, as well as that of any third-party websites, providers, or resources mentioned by the author. It is recommended that you conduct appropriate due diligence and consult with professional advisors. The author and publisher specifically disclaim any liability or loss arising from your use, application, or interpretation, directly or indirectly, of any information herein or any referenced third-party resource.

Introduction

This book will show you a safe way to predictively earn enough passive income to replace your work income and lead to your financial independence. A verse from the Eagles song, "Already Gone," says, "So often times it happens that we live our lives in chains, and we never even know we have the key." The key to your personal and financial independence is to get out of debt quickly and learn how to successfully invest on your own through undervalued blue-chip dividend paying stocks.

The best investment strategies are always simple and easy to understand. This is a little book with a large amount of information that will show you step-by-step how to invest safely in the stock market on your own, using undervalued dividend paying stocks. This book will show you how to select the best dividend stocks, give you specific examples of some of the best dividend companies, maximize your returns, minimize your taxes, and receive a never-ending flow of passive income. This becomes your new low-taxed pension plan for retirement without government control.

What's a dividend growth stock?

Put simply, a dividend growth stock is a company with a proven track record of raising its dividend (a portion of corporate profits or cash reserves paid out to shareholders) year after year. High-quality dividend growth companies typically dominate their industry, realizing steady profits and generating massive amounts of free cash flow. As a result, they're able to pay their shareholders from that cash in the form of a dividend that increases every year . . . often rising faster than the rate of inflation.

The beauty of owning a stock like this is that, no matter what happens to its share price, if the company continues to grow its dividend, then we—as shareholders—stand to collect larger and larger payouts each and every year. That's why these stocks are so compelling: you buy them when they're trading at a reasonable price, hold them, and then get showered with growing cash payouts for potentially decades to come!

Dividend investing is a slow, boring, and predictable way of becoming wealthy. Dividends create generational wealth. You will never worry about the stock price or fear the ups and downs of the market. With this strategy, you even *hope* the market goes down.

The greatest destroyer of investment wealth are expenses (advisor and mutual fund fees), taxes, inflation, misinformation, not understanding the market, and your individual emotions (fear and greed).

- When you learn to invest on your own, you will have no need for financial advisers, mutual-fund companies, and their high fees and commissions. Some of these "advisers" want to sell you complex, high-load mutual-fund investments that you don't understand. Their 1% to 3% commissions can result in a 25% to 80% lower return to you as the investor. Some advisers call themselves *wealth managers* because of the *great wealth they create for themselves.*

- Depending on what state you live in, you could pay up to 50% in taxes; it could get even higher, depending on which party is in office. This is especially true when you must take the minimum distribution draw from your 401K or other retirement investments. The tax strategies in this book will show you how to reduce or eliminate all your taxes on your investments.

- Investing in dividend paying stocks is the greatest hedge against inflation, and can be the best and safest places to put your money to beat inflation. Over the past 20 years, the inflation rate has been around 2.8%. In 2022, the inflation rate spiked to 9%, the highest inflation rate in 40 years, with no indication that it will fully subside soon.

You first need to learn how to invest on your own and know that the market always goes up over time. With a dividend investing strategy, you will care little about market price fluctuations, recognizing that, when the market drops, you can take advantage of some incredible buying opportunities.

Your focus will be to maximize your passive income through dividend growth, while minimizing your taxes through monthly qualified dividends. You will see yourself as a long-term investor like Warren Buffett, whose financial success is powered by great dividend-paying companies that he will keep forever. You will learn to buy stocks when they are undervalued and receive great passive dividend income for life.

> *"If you don't find a way to make money while*
> *you sleep, you will work until you die."*
> —WARREN BUFFETT—

Dividend example

The secret to successful investing is to have a step-by-step, simple, and safe long-term strategy that you thoroughly understand. With this investment strategy, you can retire a millionaire, but, more importantly, you will be able to *stay* a millionaire. This book will show you how to find and buy great undervalued dividend paying companies (stocks) that will produce a consistent stream of minimally taxed passive income for the rest of your life. If you take the time to learn this simple system, you will learn to make money while you sleep, so that you will have the time to live the life of your dreams. The chart below will show you what is possible:

Portfolio starting with 3% dividend yield/15% annual dividend growth/10% annual equity growth, with no additional money added, in a tax-free Roth IRA

Portfolio starting with 3% dividend yield/15% annual dividend growth/10% annual equity growth, with no additional money added, in a tax-free Roth IRA

One-Time Starting Value	10-YEAR RETURNS				20-YEAR RETURNS			
	No DRIP		DRIP		No DRIP		DRIP	
	Value	Ann Div Income	Value	Ann Div Income	Value	Ann Div Income	Value	Ann Div Income
$10,000	$26k	$1,200	$36k	$1,700	$67k	$4,900	$156k	$11,380
$50,000	$130k	$6,000	$180k	$8,400	$335k	$24.5k	$780k	$47.9k
$100,000	$260k	$12,000	$360k	$17,000	$670k	$49k	$1.56M	$114k

In this example, your portfolio starts with a 3% dividend yield. It assumes 15% annual dividend growth and 10% annual equity growth. Other than the one-time starting deposit in a tax-free Roth IRA, no additional money is added.

If you did not reinvest any of the dividends during (No DRIP), a one-time initial $10,000 investment would have grown to $67,000 after 20 years, and you would receive $4,900 in annual dividend payments that year. If you did reinvest the dividends (DRIP), an initial $10,000 investment would be worth $156,000 at year 20, and your annual dividend income would be $11,380.

By comparison, if you started with a one-time investment of $100,000 with dividends reinvested (DRIP), then, in 20 years, your portfolio would be worth $1.56 million, and you would be taking home $114,000 each year in passive income. This sounds crazy, but it is the power of compounding. If you held the stock for 30 years and got the same return, it would be worth $8,866,000 with an annual dividend income of $1,000,000 per year. This is true generational wealth.

Let's consider an example with an average investor who can put away $6,000 a year in their Roth IRA. Assume the same parameters with 3% dividend yield, 15% annual dividend growth, 10% annual equity growth, and automatically reinvest the dividends each year (DRIP). Their portfolio would be worth more-than $4 million after 30 years, and they would be taking home, tax-free, $383,000 in dividends. In 40 years, your portfolio would be worth $36,822,000 with an annual dividend income of $6.5 million That is real crazy.

Portfolio starting with 3% dividend yield/15% annual dividend growth/10% annual equity growth, with $6,000 added money each year and dividends reinvested in a tax-free Roth IRA

Starting	10-YEAR RETURNS		20-YEAR RETURNS		30-YEAR RETURNS	
	Value	Div Income	Value	Div Income	Value	Div Income
$6,000	$137,362	$6,427	$722,355	$52,720	$4,259,692	484,902

These examples were derived using a representative dividend-focused portfolio. Later in this book is a list of companies that (as of the date printed) meet the recommended guidelines you will learn about. Keep in mind that there is never any guarantee when investing in the stock market. You can use the same online calculator to review any stock's performance for the past 20 years.

https://www.marketbeat.com/dividends/calculator/

There is also a great YouTube video to show how this concept works: https://www.youtube.com/watch?v=luWaRka9L0Y

Common sense disclaimer

All books focused on investments have a disclaimer that reflects the market reality stated above: nothing in the market can be guaranteed. Therefore, it bears repeating here:

This guide is for informational and educational purposes only, based on the personal experience and research of the author. Information has been obtained from data sources considered to be reliable, but its accuracy and completeness are not guaranteed. This guide is offered with the understanding that the author and publisher are neither fiduciaries nor engaged in rendering legal, tax, investment, financial, or other advice. All content is general in nature, and your unique circumstances may include factors not considered by the author.

You assume sole responsibility for evaluating the merits and risks of the provided content, as well as that of any third-party websites, providers, or resources mentioned by the author. It is recommended that you conduct appropriate due diligence and consult with professional advisors. The author and publisher specifically disclaim any liability or loss arising from your use, application, or interpretation, directly or indirectly, of any information herein or any referenced third-party resource.

◆ ◆ ◆

Investing on Your Own

Many investors (speculators) are obsessed with the daily information about the stock market. They spend too much time watching or reading investment news and trying to analyze investments. Speculators think they can time and beat the market, while less than 10% of professional fund managers can even beat the S&P 500 over a 3-year period. Because they are speculators (gamblers) and not investors, they will continually trade instead of buying and holding onto investments. This strategy increases taxes and fees, and gobbles up profits over time.

Most novice investors buy when the price is high and sell when the price is low. They end up sitting on the sidelines during peak surges in the market. Research done by Dalbar, Inc., a company that studies investor behavior and analyzes investor market returns, consistently shows that the average investor earns below-average returns.

From January 2000 through December 2021, the S&P 500 Index averaged 7.35% a year with dividends reinvested each year. During the same period, the average equity fund investor earned a market return of only 4.25% per year. Remember, only about 10% of actively managed funds have outperformed the S&P 500 over the past 15 years. The reason for the discrepancy in returns is that the average investor loses money through advisory and mutual fund fees, and by jumping in and out of the market, influenced by their emotions.

Many individuals get confused with investing and do not understand how easy it is to invest on their own through a brokerage company like Charles Schwab. That is why they are so vulnerable to investment schemes and high-fee advisers and brokers. We seem to have an infinite capacity to stress ourselves and do stupid things, especially when it comes to money. To a large degree, this comes from greed, ego, and family encoding.

I knew one individual who took his entire retirement plan of $300,000 and put it into a real estate limited partnership. He did not understand the potential risks and rewards, and he had no control over it. Within one year, he had lost his entire retirement nest egg, which had taken him 20 years to earn. Another very smart and skilled colleague got involved in a Bernie Madoff-type Ponzi scheme and lost his entire savings of $1.3 million, which had taken him 25 years to accumulate.

"Rule No. 1 is never lose money.
Rule No. 2 is never forget Rule No. 1."
—WARREN BUFFETT—

Most individual investors put their money in mutual funds and rely upon money managers, financial advisers and brokers who engage in hyperactive trading to try to beat the market by picking winners and timing. This is a losing strategy. In most cases, investors would be better off consistently investing on their own in an S&P 500 index fund (SCHX or SPY).

The cost of advisors

Below is a real example of an actively managed mutual fund SIMPLE IRA compared to the results of the S&P 500 fund over the last 12 years. In this true example, the individual would have had $636,159 rather than $320,000 (almost twice as much) if they would have just put their investments in the S&P 500 ETF (exchange traded fund).

YEAR	BROKERAGE ACCOUNT			RETURNS		S&P 500 ACCOUNT			RETURNS	
	$ OPEN BAL	$ DEPOSITS	$ PRINCIPAL	%	$	$ OPEN BAL	$ DEPOSITS	$ PRINCIPAL	% PRETAX	$ TREATED
2009	0	7,800	7,800	-0.81%	-63		7,800	7,800	26.46%	2,064
2010	7,737	14,950	22,687	5.98%	1,357	9,864	14,950	24,814	15.06%	3,737
2011	24,044	15,400	39,444	-2.44%	-963	28,551	15,400	43,951	2.11%	927
2012	38,481	14,950	53,431	9.99%	5,339	44,878	14,950	59,828	16.00%	9,573
2013	58,770	15,600	74,370	8.56%	6,368	69,401	15,600	85,001	32.39%	27,532
2014	80,738	15,750	96,488	2.86%	2,761	112,532	15,750	128,282	13.69%	17,562
2015	99,249	15,600	114,849	-4.34%	-4,984	145,844	15,600	161,444	1.38%	2,228
2016	109,865	16,900	126,765	6.95%	8,807	163,672	16,900	180,572	11.96%	21,596
2017	135,572	18,650	154,222	12.64%	19,499	202,169	18,650	220,819	21.83%	48,205
2018	173,721	15,654	189,375	-7.26%	-13,751	269,023	15,654	284,677	-4.38%	-12,469
2019	175,624	17,046	192,670	16.67%	32,112	272,209	17,046	289,255	31.49%	91,086
2020	224,782	19,520	244,302	11.24%	27,449	380,341	19,520	399,861	18.40%	73,574
2021	271,751	20,822	292,573	9.37%	27,427	473,435	20,822	494,257	28.71%	141,901
2022	320,000		320,000			636,158		636,158		

Below is another real example of a much larger office with nine employees that has maximized all tax-deductible strategies. These are two identical plans, except one has just invested on their own in the S&P 500 compared to the investment of their financial advisor and brokerage company. They would have had more than $7 million in their 401K account instead of $2.8 million. This office lost $4,226,867 by using their financial advisors to manage their portfolio through mutual fund investments.

	BROKERAGE ACCOUNT			RETURNS		S&P 500 ACCOUNT			RETURNS	
YEAR	$ OPEN BAL	$ DEPOSITS	$ PRINCIPAL	%	$	$ OPEN BAL	$ DEPOSITS	$ PRINCIPAL	% PRETAX	$ TREATED
2009	479,897	80,000	559,897	9.81%	54,926	479,897	80,000	559,897	26.46%	148,149
2010	614,823	86,175	700,998	9.55%	66,922	708,046	86,175	794,221	15.06%	119,610
2011	767,920	86,001	853,921	-0.61%	-5,250	913,830	86,001	999,831	2.11%	21,096
2012	848,671	85,443	934,114	9.51%	88,826	1,020,928	85,443	1,106,371	16.00%	177,019
2013	1,022,940	85,673	1,108,613	10.07%	111,585	1,283,390	85,673	1,369,063	32.39%	443,440
2014	1,220,198	80,179	1,300,377	2.94%	38,289	1,812,503	80,179	1,892,682	13.69%	259,108
2015	1,338,666	81,850	1,420,516	-10.66%	-151,461	2,151,790	81,850	2,233,640	1.38%	30,824
2016	1,269,055	87,873	1,356,928	8.48%	115,049	2,264,464	87,873	2,352,337	11.96%	281,340
2017	1,471,977	88,238	1,560,215	10.13%	158,112	2,633,677	88,238	2,721,915	21.83%	594,194
2018	1,718,327	94,982	1,813,309	-6.73%	-122,059	3,316,109	94,982	3,411,091	-4.38%	-149,406
2019	1,691,250	98,899	1,790,149	12.52%	224,184	3,261,685	98,899	3,360,584	31.49%	1,058,248
2020	2,014,333	96,245	2,110,578	11.93%	251,810	4,418,832	96,245	4,515,077	18.40%	830,774
2021	2,362,388	116,383	2,478,771	13.10%	324,803	5,345,851	116,383	5,462,234	28.71%	1,568,207
2022	2,803,574		2,803,574			7,030,441		7,030,441		

I highly recommend that anyone who has a 401K plan should do a comparison **now** and not wait until they're ready to retire. On my website, I have a free Excel comparison worksheet to show how your investments have done compared to the S&P 500 fund. Go to https://www.efast.dol.gov/5500search/ and put in your EIN number to get copies of past 5500. This will show you the beginning balance and contributions you put in each year. Use these numbers to fill out the chart. This will help you realize how much you have lost or gained in your retirement account by using the various advisors and mutual funds.

- Free S&P comparison Excel calculator at https://www.doctorace.com/resources/

The late John Bogle, father of the indexed mutual fund, said in MarketWatch: "If you pay a hefty fee to an active manager, what happens to your potential return? Answer: Nothing good. At 2.5% over a typical investor's lifetime, an astounding 80% of compounding returns end up in the hands of the manager, not the investor."

He believes in index funds and says actively managed funds are a big scam. When you invest in loaded, actively managed mutual funds, you put up 100% of the capital and take 100% of the risk. If you make money, your fund manager takes up to 70% or more of the upside in fees. If you lose money, they still get paid. They are charging you 10 to 30 times what it would cost for you to buy a low-cost index fund that would match the market and beat 90% of the actively managed mutual funds.

Expenses and fees are the enemy of the individual investor. You must understand that advisors, brokers, and mutual fund managers are well meaning salespeople. They charge 1% to 4% of your entire portfolio even when you lose money. They will take 50% to 80% of your gains.

If you invest on your own in an index S&P 500 fund at $4,000 per month for 30 years at 7% return, you will earn $3,781,475. What will your financial advisors and mutual fund take from your earnings when they charge only 1%, 2%, 3%, or 4% fees?

ADVISORY/FUND % FEE	THE MONEY ADVISORY/FUND WILL TAKE FROM YOU	% RETURN OF YOUR EARNINGS
1%	$962,322	25%
2%	$1,725,989	46%
3%	$2,332,220	62%
4%	$2,820,600	75%

As you can see in the chart above, they will take from you up to 75% of your earnings. They will get their fees even when you lose money that year.

"Unfortunately, the vast majority of those who bill themselves as financial advisors neither charge a fair price nor give good advice. More than any other market I know, the market for financial advice is 'Let the buyer beware.'"
—JIM DAHLE, M.D.

Remember, the person who cares the most about your money is you. Learn to invest on your own, and stay away from financial advisers and brokers who work on commission.

Prioritizing your money

If you have debt or a mortgage, the primary focus of your excess money should be in debt reduction. However, take 10% of that money and learn how to invest in the dividend investing strategy now. You will learn how to invest with a small amount of money while helping build your confidence and trust in this method. Once you are debt free in 5 to 10 years, with your home paid off and a steady income, most of your net worth is now in inflation-adjusted, secure "bond-like" assets. Now you can focus 60% to 70% of your earnings into creating a significant dividend portfolio.

The price of homes today is out of the reach of many Americans. To reach financial freedom, they should initially only rent a conservative home or apartment and focus excess money toward a dividend investing portfolio. This will save thousands of dollars that they would have given to the bank in home mortgage interest payments. Doing this over time will make you very wealthy so that eventually you can purchase the home of your dreams.

You now need less money to live and can manage any significant market downturn that would last four to five years. You will never have a need to sell your stocks. Remember, during downturns—these are the times to buy.

You must remember two things when investing in dividend stocks. First, you must believe in long-term success of American business, and second, the money you invest in the market should be money that you don't need for the next five years, preferably 10 years. These dividend paying stocks will keep producing passive income every month, with increasing returns every year. The equity value will grow over time, leading to incredible wealth and security. These stocks will eventually pay you more money passively than you earn in your job. You will never have to worry about money again. It is that simple.

Even if you start later in life and enter retirement debt-free, you will have plenty of abundance through your 401K, pension income, Social Security, dividend investing income, and most of your healthcare costs will be covered by Medicare. You will easily be able to manage any long-term market drops because your retirement money and dividends from income-producing stocks will allow you to live very well. This will allow you to always keep your money in your dividend investing blue-chip stocks to continue a constant flow of low-tax income. You will never have to sell your stocks to live but will be able to pass them on to your children or charities as your legacy.

If you need access to funds for an emergency, you can gain easy access with paid off credit or a Health Savings Account (HSA), which can usually be accessed tax-free. **When you are completely debt-free, how much money do you need to live?**

Learning to invest

Many brokers and financial advisors want to make investing sound difficult and complicated so that you must rely upon them for advice. Investing is quite simple if you focus on investments that are easily understood and give you the highest performance. In this book, I will show you some of those investments and give you a step-by-step approach to selecting the right investments and how to purchase them.

Learning to invest today is not complicated and will not take you long to learn. **Start now!** Set up a brokerage account with Charles Schwab, and learn a simple, step-by-step approach to selecting and buying the best investments. Start with small investments first to build your knowledge and confidence.

* Get started here: https://www.schwab.com 800-435-4000

The best investment in the market that you can make is to buy undervalued blue-chip qualified dividend paying stocks. With these, you will create a constant, growing stream of passive income that continues to increase over time. These great dividend stocks always continue to produce great income, even during bear markets.

Warren Buffett buys great companies at great prices (undervalued blue-chip qualified dividend paying stocks) and holds them forever. He believes in the "coffee can" approach to investing. He keeps his stocks in a "coffee can" and never plans to sell them, even when they are at their all-time highs. Many times, these companies will continually grow higher. Selling stocks at an all-time high is like trading Michael Jordan when he is the highest team scorer. Sell a stock only when the company cuts or stops paying their dividends.

To invest in the stock market without emotions, you must first change your investment philosophy and focus. Your primary focus needs to be on the dividend growth and your increasing dividend income, and secondarily on dividend yield. High-quality companies with long-term histories of consistent dividend increases acquired at undervalue will be the winners in all market environments. The increasing income with dividend growth will provide sufficient cash to meet current and future spending needs and protect you from inflation. The capital appreciation of these companies is just an added bonus.

When do you need to hire a financial advisor?

If you don't have the time, interest, or skills to buy dividend stocks on your own, then a financial advisor who is paid by the hour and not on commission may be able to help build a solid portfolio of strong dividend companies. The main reason you hire an advisor is to help you stay in the market when the market is down. When your stocks drop in value by 20%, a good advisor will keep you in the market, preventing you from making a bad decision.

Most financial advisors are honest and extremely hardworking; they try their best for their clients. The problem is they are working on an old paradigm of investing. They like diversification between U.S. and international stocks, mitigating safety through bonds, and trying to beat the market through extensive research. In most cases, they do not do as well as the S&P 500. And in most cases, the S&P 500 does not do as well as high quality dividend paying stocks. This is especially true in down markets.

It's important to note that not all financial advisors are the same. Only use an hourly fee fiduciary financial planner who is an expert in dividend investing. They can help you learn how to invest in dividend stocks and give you tax-planning help. Fiduciary advisors are professionally obligated to make investment decisions with your best interests in mind.

Non-fiduciary advisors may recommend products for which they receive a big commission or other forms of payment, and they don't have the same professional obligation to act in your best interests.

◆ ◆ ◆

Understanding Market Volatility

The stock market is the only place where customers run out of the store during a big sale. When the stock market drops and we see our portfolio being reduced, our fight-or-flight emotions are stimulated. Long-term dividend investors are overjoyed rather than depressed when the market is down, realizing the great opportunities they have been given by this market drop. During these times, your dividend payments usually go up and provide you more money to live on. This is what you need to remember during downturns in the market.

Here are some great Warren Buffett quotes:

- "Opportunities of a 15% to 30% bear market drop rarely occur, and when they do, you need to buy as much of the good undervalued dividend blue-chip companies as you can while they are on sale."

- "Whether we're talking about socks or stocks, I like buying quality merchandise when it is marked down."

- "If you can detach yourself from the crowd and become greedy while others are fearful, you can become very rich, and you don't have to be smart. It does not take brains; it takes temperament."

- "Every decade or so, dark clouds will fill the economic skies, and they will briefly rain gold!"

Remind yourself you are debt-free, that you have a constant source of income, and that these great opportunities occur only a few times in your life. Start rounding up more cash, and hope the market drops further for even greater opportunities. Remember that you have invested in great companies that do well in tough times. You are now able to buy more shares of those companies at great prices.

Bear markets

Below is a chart of the average historical corrections of the S&P 500 Composite Index from 1948 to 2017:

Average Historical Corrections of the Market

	REGULAR DECLINE (5% OR MORE)	MODEST CORRECTION (10% OR MORE)	SERIOUS CORRECTION (15% OR MORE)	BEAR MARKET (20% OR MORE)
FREQUENCY	3 times/year	1 time/year	Every 3.5 years	Every 6.3 years
AVERAGE LOSS BEFORE DROP ENDS	11%	19%	27%	35%
AVERAGE DURATION	46 days	117 days	275 days	425 days

In Tony Robbins book *Unshakeable*, he states that, over the past 70 years, there have been only 14 bear markets, averaging one every five years, lasting an average of one year, and ranging from 45 days to nearly two years. He says that what you need to know is that bear markets don't last and are always followed by a bull market during the next 12 months. From March 9, 2009, the S&P 500 index surged by 69.5% over the next 12 months.

Since 2009, there was a 17% drop in 2010 and an 18% drop in 2011. Since then, we have had only 12 corrections in the S&P 500 that were greater than 10%. 2018 was a very volatile year, with drops of 7%, 10% and 19.3%. This is probably because of the ending of the Federal Reserve's policy of quantitative easing from 2009 to 2014 and low interest rates, forcing more investors into the market.

In 2020 during COVID, it was a great year to test your risk tolerance and an excellent year to buy stocks at the bottom during our only bear market (20% or more drop) since 2009. The 2020 bear market began on February 14, 2020, resulting in a 32.2% drop until its low on March 23, 2020. What a wonderful time to buy. From December 2021, the market has rebounded with a more-than 114% increase from its low in March 2020.

Our most recent correction occurred from January 3, 2022, until the low on October 14, 2022, where we had an total drop in the S&P 500 of -27.5%. By the end of the year 2022, the S&P 500 finished at -18.11% down, including dividends reinvested, while my dividend portfolio of 25 stocks, which grew by 7.17%. This is the power of a great dividend portfolio.

Your account had a rate of return of 7.17% from Jan 1, 2022 to Dec 30, 2022.

How is this calculated?

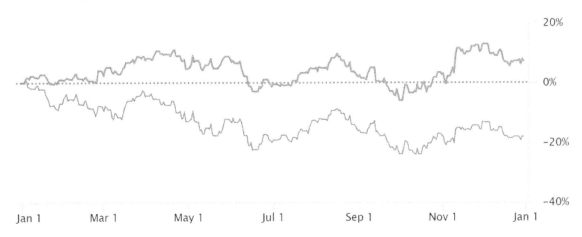

When you purchase S&P 500, there will be many companies that are average or below average, some that are above average, and some that have exceptional growth. By selecting the best companies (those which have increased dividends for more than 10 years) your returns can be 3% to 4% higher than the average return of the S&P 500.

Remember, short-term volatility is a long-term opportunity. Another way to look at it? Short-term pain is long-term gain. You only lose in down markets when you sell. You win in a down market when you buy!

Historically, there are corrections during election years. Some say that, in May and June, the market is higher but down in September and October. Mark Twain said "October is one of the peculiarly dangerous months to speculate in stocks. The others are July, January, September, April, November, May, March, June, December, August, and February."

Dealing with your investment emotions

The second greatest enemy of the investor is being controlled by fear and emotion. When you are invested in great companies, getting out of the market when it starts to drop is a big mistake. This is the time you need to buy more stocks in those great dividend paying companies.

As humans, we are wired with a fight-or-flight emotional base. Our emotions make life worth living, but uncontrolled emotions while investing can be deadly. If you are unable to tolerate or cannot discipline and control your emotions when there is a 10%, 20%, or even 40% drop in the market, then you should place your money in a **Personal Bank** (high cash value whole life insurance) and not worry about the market. A well-designed high cash value whole life insurance will grow tax-deferred at 3% to 4%, beating inflation, and you will be able to access the money tax-free.

- For more information about personal banks: https://ibcglobalinc.com/

Dick Collier said, "If your investment portfolio is keeping you awake at night, sell down to the sleeping point." Warren Buffett says you must treat your investments as if it is a family farm and check on it only once a month. You would not sell your farm, but you would continually buy more land to extend the yields on your crops. Your dividend income is just like income from rental properties with fewer headaches.

Great investors spend little time watching or worrying about the market. They are debt-free and have a constant source of income from their job and/or dividend returns. Because of this, they worry little about a long-lasting bear market. They are invested in diverse sectors of great blue-chip dividend paying companies that they will not sell, knowing these companies will always rebound from down markets. With these companies, you are getting a positive increase of income every year which is not dependent on the price of the stock.

Great investors look at the market and their investments only once a month for about an hour. When they have cash in their brokerage account, they search for undervalued blue-chip companies from the dividend achievers in this book or the IQT newsletter (described later). These savvy investors follow the safe and simple investing game plan, and they stick with it. This prevents them from doing stupid things with their money such as investing in long shots or other investments they know nothing about. They have patience, available cash, and courage, and always respond with logic instead of a knee-jerk reaction. They rarely listen to the financial news throughout the year.

There are many advantages to selecting great dividend companies and holding them forever. These are large companies that generate the strongest returns of any major asset class over the long run. The cost of buying and selling individual securities is free now—and holding stocks after purchasing them is free. When you use Schwab, there are no buying or selling fees on these dividend paying companies. The stock market's combination of transparency (readily available financials) and liquidity reduce uncertainty relative to more opaque and illiquid investments such as real estate.

The big drawback of the stock market for most retirees is volatility, but for the long-term dividend investor, volatility isn't a drawback but a gigantic advantage. When your portfolio produces the income you need, if stock prices fall by 10% or even 50%, your dividend income doesn't fall (assuming you are in strong businesses that always increase their dividend) because dividend income is not impacted by stock declines.

Dividends vs. stock price

The graph below plots Johnson and Johnson's (JNJ) stock price against its dividend per share. Each year the company's dividend grew 6% to 10%, even though JNJ's stock price fell 40% during the 2007–09 financial crisis and has experienced other prolonged periods of stagnation or decline. During this time, Johnson and Johnson (JNJ) continued to provide reliable, increasing annual income to their investors while preserving their purchasing power. Note how the dividend increases has pushed the share price upward over time.

When the market drops 20% to 50% is when you use your dividend returns to buy more undervalued blue-chip dividend paying stocks. Normally we are cautious about buying dividend blue-chip stocks that are paying more than 6%. The exception is during deep market downturns when great companies that normally pay dividends at 1% to 3% can be bought at a discount and lock in incredible dividend yields of 3% to 8%. An example today is the dividend king Stanley, Black and Decker (SWK).

Another example is Whirlpool (WHR) founded in 1929, with today's price of $142 per share with a dividend yield of 4.93%. However, during the COVID crisis in April 2020, the price was $88 per share, and you would have locked in a dividend yield of 5.47%. Over the next 2 years, your return on your Whirlpool investment due to equity growth is nearly 2 times. These companies have stood the test of time and will always rebound.

JOHNSON & JOHNSON: DIVIDEND VS. STOCK PRICE

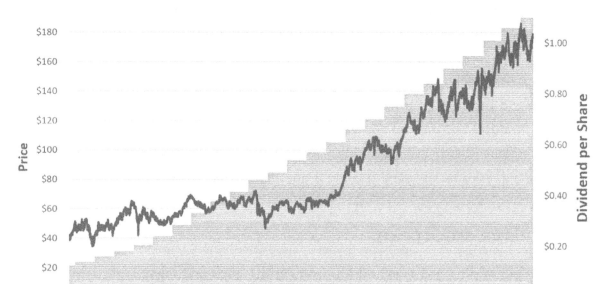

Take advantage of these bear markets. The only time you sell is when they cut or stop paying dividends. During a nasty bear market, some stocks may go down as much as 50%, but please don't give in to your fear and sell. You will immediately lose your dividend income. Turn off your computer, and don't even look at where they are trading. Even better, add some fresh cash to your account, and buy more of them when they are down.

If you buy a stock when it is down 50% from its high, and it returns to its old high, you will have made not 50%, but 100% on your money.

All the companies listed at the end of this book have either increased or maintained their dividend rate through the last recession. It is very rare that any of these companies will cut their dividends. You can set up an alert in a Charles Schwab account to notify you of dividend increases or cuts.

◆　◆　◆

Market Timing

On *July 15, 2021, Schwab Center* for Financial Research published a study entitled "Does Market Timing Work?" They considered the performance of five hypothetical long-term investors following very different investment strategies. Each received $2,000 at the beginning of every year for the 20 years ending in 2020 and left the money in the stock market, as represented by the S&P 500 Index. Check out how they fared:

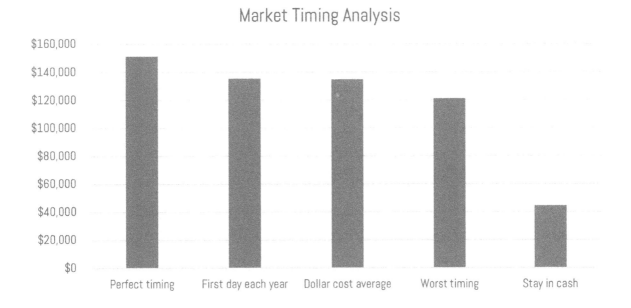

- The first scenario was **perfect market timing**, and they invested their full $2000 each year exactly at the lowest closing of each year. After 20 years, their final return was **$151,391**.

- The second scenario was to just invest the $2000 in the market the **first day of the year,** resulting in a return of **$135,471**—only $15,920 less than the perfect timing scenario.

- The third scenario was **cost dollar averaging** where the $2000 was divided into 12 equal portions and invested at the beginning of each month. This approach earned third place with **$134,856** at the end of 20 years.

- The fourth scenario was investing at the **poorest timing** each year at the peak of the market. The poor timing resulted in the return of **$121,171,** just $14,300 short of the second-best scenario.

- The 5th and worst scenario **stayed in cash investments** (using Treasury bills as a proxy) for the 20 years while waiting for the right opportunity to buy stocks—but never bought. This resulted in a return of only **$44,438**, which is just one-third of the return of the other four scenarios!

Conclusion: Investing and staying in the market using the S&P 500 index, even when you bought at the worst time, will give you **three times (3X) greater investment return over time** compared to cash (treasuries/bond) investments. The greatest advantage that you have in the stock market is **time** and **compound interest.**

*Time in the market is much more
important than timing the market.*

The biggest mistake you can make

The biggest mistake is not getting into the market. On October 14, 2022, the market has dropped 27.5% from its January 3, 2022, all-time high. Interest rates are historically low, inflation is at its highest point in 40 years, the U.S. has significant debt, and there is a war in Ukraine.

This bad news has created an environment where many high-quality dividend paying stocks are trading at a discount, and a low price will provide great value for small investors. It is much harder for Warren Buffett and large mutual fund managers to find great deals in an overvalued market.

Don't try to time the market, but take what the market gives you. A common mistake that many investors make is waiting for the best time to buy instead of looking for the best undervalued stock at that time. The IQT newsletter will tell you which stocks are undervalued and what price to pay for them. When the stock market is at all-time highs, you may be able to buy only a few companies on sale. This is the time to use "good until canceled" limit orders set at prices that are undervalued for your desired company. In October 2022, June 2022, and March 2020, the stock market dropped more than 20%, which would enable you to fill up your wish list of 20 dividend stocks that you will keep forever.

The only time you need to look at your stock portfolio is once a month when you have cash in your brokerage account from your automatic bank deposits or dividends. Go through your watch list, and purchase those stocks that day if they are undervalued. Now you will start earning income today from those companies, because you plan to keep these companies forever.

> *"Only buy something that you'd be perfectly happy*
> *to hold if the market shut down for 10 years."*
> —WARREN BUFFETT—

Dividend Aristocrats

You are more successful as a long-term investor because it puts your focus on what matters: the success of a business. If you invest for the long run, you will focus on businesses with strong and durable competitive advantages. Importantly, there are dividend-paying businesses that have historically outperformed the market over time such as the dividend aristocrats. These are made up of 68 stocks exclusively with 25+ years of rising dividends that meet certain minimum size and liquidity requirements.

During the 10-year period ending in September 2016, the S&P Dividend Aristocrats have indexed an average annual rate of return of 10.14% while the S&P 500 Index has returned an average annualized rate of return of just 7.22% during the lost decade around the Great Recession. Usually, higher returns indicate higher risk, but the Aristocrats have achieved their returns with less volatility and less risk than the S&P 500.

When you understand that you are in the market to receive a passive income through dividends as well as equity growth over time, you don't worry about the ups and downs of the market. Investing safely and smartly in the stock market is your greatest hedge against inflation and will allow you to create incredible wealth for your retirement years.

During the COVID crash in 2020, my friend continued to stay in the market and continued to buy undervalued blue-chip stocks while they were on sale. Over the next two years, his net worth increased by 20% as the market rebounded. A friend of his got out of the market completely and was bragging how smart he was but failed to get back into the market and missed out on the 114% rebound of the S&P 500 over the next year.

Market timing is a loser strategy. If you really believe in America and that the market will always go up over time as it has always done, you stay in the market. The only time you sell a stock is when the company cuts or stops paying dividends. You sell that stock the next day and reinvest that money back into another great dividend paying stock.

◆ ◆ ◆

How to Invest on Your Own Through Charles Schwab

W*hen you learn to invest on your own,* you become the chess player/master instead of the chess piece. With the internet, investing in the market on your own is very simple. First, open a brokerage account with Charles Schwab.

Why Charles Schwab?

I have no connection with Charles Schwab, other than I like and use their services. They have low or no fees for trading stocks, a user-friendly interface, and incredible customer service. It is an American multinational financial services company. It offers banking, commercial banking, an electronic trading platform, and wealth management advisory services to both retail and institutional clients. It has more than 360 branches, primarily in financial centers in the United States and the United Kingdom. It is the 13th largest banking institution in the United States, with more than $6.6 trillion in client assets. It is one of the three-largest asset managers in the world.

Charles Schwab is open 24 hours a day, 7 days a week, and has excellent representatives and brokers. Schwab also requires no dollar minimums to open an account, it has the lowest expense ratios, and when you buy stocks and index ETFs (exchange-traded funds), there are no trading fees, compared to many other companies.

While Schwab was designed to sell stocks and provide stock investors with the most current and useful information, they offer everything that any big bank would offer, including checking and savings accounts. They also have great trading platforms. There are no commissions for any stocks or ETF trades.

All representatives and Schwab brokers are salaried; they do not work on commission, so their advice focuses on your best interests. Schwab has agents located in most large cities. These local Schwab brokers can help you open an account, but it may be easier to go online and have an account set up within 30 minutes. You can call their online representative (800-435-4000) to help you through this process.

- Set up your Charles Schwab account: https://www.schwab.com/client-home

Once you set up an account, you'll then need to "fund" your Charles Schwab cash account (not margin account) by linking it to your personal bank accounts. Call up a Schwab representative to help you create this link. Within a day, you will be able to transfer money from your own bank account into your Schwab investment account. Once it is set up, then transfer the amount of money you plan to invest. You can also set up an automatic transfer each month if you would like. Another option is to just send a check to Schwab. Check with a representative to verify the correct address to send the check, and write your name and account number on the check. After your brokerage account is set up, download the Charles Schwab app on your phone.

Working with Charles Schwab

Working with your Schwab representative, you can easily transfer stocks and funds from your old brokerage account into your Schwab account without even talking to your high-paid advisor in the other brokerage house. It is almost always better to sell your mutual funds from the other brokerage house through Schwab because there are no fees. You can also create IRA accounts through Schwab and transfer your 401K assets into that account.

Most likely you will have many mutual funds and non-paying dividend companies in your past account. You may be afraid to sell some of these companies when the stock market is down for fear of taking a loss. Don't be afraid to sell these companies and poorly returning mutual funds for great undervalued dividend paying companies that are also down in price. You are just trading one poor company or mutual fund for a greater company that pays a great dividend at a low price.

Once your account is funded, you will be all ready to trade. Call up your Schwab representative, and have them walk you through a step-by-step process to buy stocks. You may want to go to YouTube and watch some of the videos that talk about beginning your Schwab account.

Next, start investing using the strategies I describe. I also recommend becoming familiar with the Charles Schwab website, especially the area of research. Click the "Research" tab, and then hit "Stocks" and type in the ticker symbol of the stock you want to research.

- Charles Schwab research: https://client.schwab.com/app/research/

This section of the website has numerous free research newsletters that will describe individual companies, give performance data, and the outlook for the coming year. They also give you important data about your dividends and payout ratios. Below is an example showing dividend growth and equity growth with Texas Instruments over the past eight years:

Other great websites for research include:
https://www.marketbeat.com/stocks/
https://www.digrin.com/
https://www.morningstar.com/
https://finance.yahoo.com/

For serious dividend investors, my favorite paid subscription website is Simply Safe Dividends. Simply Safe Dividends provides a suite of portfolio tracking tools, research, and time-tested Dividend Safety Scores trusted by thousands of income investors. The platform helps investors avoid dividend cuts, keep their dividend portfolios between the guardrails, discover new ideas, and stay informed—without the noise and sensationalism found at many other financial websites. Within minutes, you can transfer all your brokerage accounts into this website to do detail analysis. Their annual fee is $499 per year to subscribe.

- Subscription option: www.simplysafedividends.com

Tips to get started with dividend investing

Initially, start with a small amount (let's say $1000) and practice buying dividend stocks in your Schwab account. Spread your purchases over 6 to 12 companies off the list provided later in this book. Buy those that are the most undervalued. You may want to call up the Schwab representative to help you through your initial trades.

Once you are debt-free, you will be easily able to put 20% to 30% of your income into your Schwab account. Set up an automatic transfer from your bank each month so that a portion of your income funds your account.

You can use the dividends to live on, or, if you are still working, it would be better to reinvest the dividends automatically. You can have them automatically reinvested into that same stock or put into cash in your Schwab account. To accelerate the growth of your portfolio, continually add money to your Schwab account each month. Use this additional money to buy more stock shares in great undervalued dividend companies. Once you have started, check your portfolio each month, and continue to buy undervalued stocks. The only time you will sell a stock is when the company cuts their dividends.

Schwab also has an area where you can check your portfolio growth compared to the S&P 500 to see how you're doing:

- Schwab S&P comparison: https://client.schwab.com/app/portfoliohealth/#/

To check how much dividend income you are getting from these companies, go to the tab "Investment Income" in your Schwab account. This will give you the dollar amount you will receive each month and for the entire year. Take that number, and divide it by the value of what you initially paid for the stocks (your cost basis expense: what you paid for the stocks, not what the stocks are worth now). In just a few years, your initial 2.5% dividend yield can double to 5% and eventually up to 10 or 15% over the years with these great, safe companies.

Remember, those who become extremely wealthy do six things:

- They never become enslaved by debt and pay off all their debts early.

- They spend their money wisely, getting maximum value for every dollar.

- They continuously work to increase both their active and their passive incomes.

- They are aggressive savers, allowing them to pay off debt early while learning to invest.

- They take the time to learn how to manage their investments on their own. They are disciplined investors who find a good strategy, and they stick with it. They started investing early, safely, and sanely, and avoided making the big mistakes that may take years to make up.

- Because of their wealth they are extremely generous and give back to society.

◆ ◆ ◆

Why Buy Undervalued Dividend-Paying Blue-Chip Stocks?

In the real estate market, your return is in property's equity growth and rental income. In bonds, CDs, and the money market, it is interest. In the stock market, it is equity growth, but, more importantly, it is the stream of income from dividends.

Over the last 40 years, 71% of the S&P500 returns have come from dividends, not capital appreciation. You should never own stocks that don't pay a dividend. There is greater volatility around companies that don't pay dividends because there is no cushion against the yield. The only reason to own stock is to get free cash flow. Each year, you need to evaluate the strength of the company to be able to generate a great dividend while maintaining and increasing its equity value. Charlie Munger said, "If it has no cash flow, just say no!!"

Those who ignore the importance of dividends in making stock market selections are not investors. They are called "speculators." Speculators hope that the price of a stock will go up and reward them with profits. Great investors focus on dividend returns, knowing eventually all great companies will go up over time. Meanwhile, they are getting a return on their capital.

Michael Alexander wrote in his book entitled *Stock Cycles* that, since 1802, there have been 8 long-term bear markets and 8 long-term bull markets. The last long-term bear market we called "The Lost Decade," and it was from the year 2000 to the year 2013. For those 13 years, the value of the S&P 500 fund did not increase beyond the price in year 2000. Dividend investors not only survived but thrived during this lost decade, because they continually saw their income increase every year, with no need to sell any of their stocks. Sleeping well at night is one of the true advantages to dividend investing.

Speculators and retirees living off their mutual fund 401K investments without dividend income fear long-term bear markets. Knowledgeable dividend investors love this time because they know they will continue to receive increasing dividends and income every year. They also can buy great dividend-paying blue-chip companies on sale (undervalued).

In 2002 and 2009, during those 50% market drops, many great dividend-paying companies' stocks dropped, and you could buy them for half price. During this same time, their dividend yield and dividend income significantly increased. Even more importantly, dividend income usually increases during these turbulent times in the market with great companies.

Dividend growth vs. stock price

Even when the market is flat, long-term dividend investors will see their dividend income increasing each year. They do not care about the price of the stock, because **dividend income is not connected to stock price:**

McDonald's (MCD) $16/share in 2000 and $268/share 2022 (21-year range $16 to $264) Div paid since 1976											
Year	2000	2001	2002	2003	2004	2005	2006	2007	2008	2009	2010
Dividend	$0.22	$0.23	$0.24	$0.40	$0.55	$0.67	$1.00	$1.50	$1.55	$2.00	$2.26
1000 shares	$220	$230	$240	$400	$550	$670	$1,000	$1,500	$1,550	$2,000	$2,260
%Yield on cost	1.38%	1.44%	1.50%	2.50%	3.44%	4.19%	6.25%	9.38%	9.69%	12.50%	14.13%
Price/share	$16	$17	$14	$12	$17	$19	$23	$32	$38	$35	$50
Year	2011	2012	2013	2014	2015	2016	2017	2018	2019	2020	2021
Dividend	$2.53	$2.87	$3.12	$3.28	$3.44	$3.61	$3.83	$4.19	$4.73	$5.00	$5.21
1000 shares	$2,530	$2,870	$3,120	$3,280	$3,440	$3,610	$3,830	$4,190	$4,730	$5,000	$5,210
%Yield on cost	15.81%	17.94%	19.50%	20.50%	21.50%	22.56%	23.94%	26.19%	29.56%	31.25%	32.56%
Price/share	$61	$70	$75	$77	$83	$103	$131	$150	$183	$190	$264

Those who bought McDonald's in the year 2000 for $16/share were getting 1.38% dividend yield. Their dividend yield on original cost will increase each year because of the yearly dividend growth. In one year alone, 2021, they **earned 32.25% dividend yield** on the original share price they bought 21 years before. This is called "yield on cost" and is based on the original $16/share price at the time of purchase in the year 2000. Just think: a 32% yearly return from a great company is simply amazing. In 2000, you were getting $220 in dividends, but, in 2021, the same 1000 shares are giving you $5,160 a year from dividends. Also, those 1000 shares you bought for $16,000 are now worth $264,000 (February 2023).

Even if McDonald's share price remained the same for those 20 years, you still would have received $52,430 in dividends on your initial $16,000 investment. This is a return of more than three times on your money.

McDonald's dividend increased every year, as did the percentage of dividend yield on the original shares, even in a bear market. Look at the significant 24% dividend increase in the year 2009, even when McDonald's share price dropped. This also occurred in 2002 and 2003. During those 21 years, the total dividend growth was **23.5 times**, with an annualized rate of return on dividends of **16.2%**.

One of the nicest things about this strategy is its low maintenance—less than one hour a month to reinvest the dividends or add more stocks with new money. If you automatically reinvest the dividends or spend them each month, there is no need to look at your portfolio. The only time you will sell those companies is when you get a dividend alert that they will be cutting their dividends. Then you sell the stock the next day.

With this constant source of passive income, you will no longer worry about just living on Social Security and selling your stocks in your 401K to live on during your retirement years. Dividend investing becomes your best pension plan. Your dividend income increases every year faster than inflation through the process of dividend growth. This will provide great retirement income without selling any of your stocks. More importantly, there are no advisor or mutual fund fees. In addition, if you have your money in a non-deferred account, there will be no government control or 401K-distribution taxes.

Dividend stocks make compelling investments to build and grow your retirement income portfolio. That's because:

- Stocks offer both income and appreciation potential.

- Dividend growth stocks offer potential rising income over time.

- Stocks have outperformed other asset classes over the long run by a wide margin.

- Individual stocks give you the ability to target the yield, growth, and safety you need.

- Individual stocks don't have wealth-reducing fees like funds do.

Recommended reading and viewing

To help you better understand dividend investing, I would highly recommend three books for you to read.

Dividend Investing Made Easy, **by Matthew R. Kratter**

This is a very easy read; it explains the concept of dividends clearly, and there is also an e-book and Audible edition on Amazon. Below is a short summary of his book. In his book, he recommended using Robinhood as a broker, which he no longer uses and now recommends more full-service companies such as Schwab.

He refers to dividends from stocks as "little cash machines." Every three months, they spit out cash. The beauty of dividend investing is that it's simple, powerful, and one of the best proven ways to build extreme wealth. It's always better to have your money work for you, rather than you work for money.

This investment strategy is not just for the rich, but everyone. You can learn to replace your work income through dividend investing and become financially independent. Kratter gives an example in his book of Ronald Read, who spent the first half of his life as a gas-station attendant and then the rest of his life as a janitor at his local J.C. Penney department store.

When he died in 2014 at the age of 92, he left behind an $8 million fortune, all of it in dividend-paying stocks. Today the value would have grown to $16 million. If you assume an average 3% dividend yield across his portfolio, he was collecting $20,000 every month in dividends at the time of his death.

When you buy a share of stock, you become a partial owner of the business. As a partial owner, you are entitled to a share of the profits that the business generates. Most mature companies will do two things with their profits. They will reinvest some of their profits back into the business to grow it and return some of their profits to the owners. Profits (cash) that are returned to the owners are called "dividends."

Companies that offer dividends pay a fixed amount per share and can adjust it up or down with each earnings period (usually a calendar quarter), based on how the company is doing. If you own a dividend-paying stock, you will usually get paid a dividend every three months. This dividend payment will show up as a cash deposit into your brokerage account. This cash is yours to keep, use, or reinvest back into more undervalued dividend-paying blue-chip stocks.

Dividend Growth Machine: How to Build a Worry-Free Retirement with Dividend Stocks, **by Nathan Winklepleck**

This book is also available on Audible, and I recommend that you check out his great Youtube Videos:

- Winklepleck video: https://www.youtube.com/watch?v=luWaRka9L0Y

The following are excerpts from his book, which gives the 10 reasons why you need to learn to invest on your own and stay away from advisors and Wall Street's mutual fund managers.

1. *No mutual fund fees*

2. *Direct ownership*

3. *Higher income*

4. *Own higher quality stocks*

5. *Dividend stocks outperform non-dividend-paying stocks*

6. *Think longer term*

7. *Minimal or no trading costs compared to mutual funds*

8. *Lower taxes*

9. *Ignore Mr. Market*

10. *Get 100% of your dividend income*

Nathan also says that research has shown that near-term price momentum over the past 3 to 18 months tends to continue. In other words, a stock that has been falling in value for the past year will likely continue to fall. This doesn't always hold, but plenty of academic papers confirm this phenomenon.

The lesson for you is clear: Don't try to "catch a falling knife." A "falling knife" is a stock that has been declining in price dramatically. Rather than buying them on the way down, it can be a good practice to put them on a "watch list" until the price starts to show some stability or upward movement. These companies can often present good long-term opportunities, but near-term trends can be hard to break. From November 2021 to October 2022, T. Rowe Price (TROW) dropped in half from $221 per share to a price of $93 per share from before it started to rebound. During that time, it still paid and increased its dividends.

Using some simple moving averages can help you with this. For example, let's say you identify a stock you really like—but the price is heading straight down. Put it on a list. When the stock price rises above, say, the 50- or 200-day moving average—consider buying it.

The Single Best Investment: Creating Wealth with Dividend Growth, by Lowell Miller

This is a must-read book, and here's a short summary with the emphasis on the rules of picking the right dividend stocks:

History has shown that stocks are the right investments for all environments that include inflation. Safe investments such as T-bills, bonds, CDs, and money-market funds are poor investments because what they give is less than inflation takes away.

Investing is not about playing the market—it's about becoming a partner in a business. Create a compounding machine—don't play the market. Even annual dividend income returns of 10% can produce gains of nearly 600% in 20 years. Time is all you need. Time and a sensible investment that makes maximum use of compounding.

The operator is just as important as the machine. Dividend growth is the energy that drives the compounding machine. Dividend growth pushes up the price of the stock and is the true signal of a prospering company. Stock prices should theoretically rise in a percentage increment equal to the amount of dividend growth. This applies to stocks with above-average yields.

Reinvestment of dividends brings you more and more shares, each of which earns dividends and is subject to the effect of dividend growth. Compounding with reinvested dividends has an astronomical effect over time.

The dividend investing strategy provides a framework, but true success depends upon maintaining a calm and passive attitude. Emotions and unnecessary decisions are the undoing of most investors. Hold your stocks as if they were real estate, with a cold, objective eye, an eye fixed on the horizon. Sell if dividends are cut, or it appears the dividend may not be increased, or if too much time passes without an increase and there's no legitimate excuse for a failure to increase.

A single best dividend investment portfolio is intended to replace a balanced or asset allocation portfolio, and shows nearly identical risk characteristics but without the performance drag of a fixed income (bonds and CDs). Diversify among 5 to 6 sectors with 15 to 25 different stocks. All positions should be at equal dollar weighting. You can tilt the portfolio toward higher current income, depending on your needs; you may give up some capital appreciation, but, in many markets, you may not.

It is a simple formula: high-quality undervalued dividend-paying companies + high current yield + high growth of yield = high total return.

Manic-depressive market

It's helpful to think of the market as a manic-depressive that causes the prices of stocks to move up and down every day. This can even happen to great dividend paying companies, even though the actual value of the business does not change much during these market up and down swings.

Jason Fieber says,

"It comes down to price versus value. Price is what you pay, but value is what you get. Outside of some major event, a business isn't going to suddenly be worth a lot more or a lot less on Tuesday than it was on Monday. And so, if the price of equity in a great business drops significantly, even while the value of that equity hasn't dropped significantly, that could be a fantastic opportunity to jump in for the long term.

"This is especially true when dealing with dividend growth stocks, because, all else equal, price and yield are inversely correlated. When the price drops, the yield rises. And this gets you that much closer to living off of the dividends your investments provide for you. Plus, you're usually looking at better long-term total return when starting from a lower valuation. It's more for less."

Check out his YouTube videos:

https://www.youtube.com/watch?v=BaM9o6Q5a0E
https://www.youtube.com/watch?v=L_mlFNaZ-nw

In the video, Jason Fieber also gives the five reasons to invest in dividend growth stocks:

- Reliability.

- Passive income.

- Guide you to the best businesses on the planet. It filters out lower quality companies. It shows you which companies can afford to pay a dividend. It shows you which companies value their shareholders enough to share their profits with them.

- It gives you passive income that grows every year faster than inflation.

- It beats the market over the long run.

Jason also addressed the following questions:

What are the most important key indicators for selecting a great company?

"There's a framework I use which basically breaks things down into quantitative analysis (fundamentals), qualitative analysis (opportunities, competitive advantages), risks, and valuation. When I think of a quality company, I'm thinking of a high degree of secular of revenue and profit growth, a very long track record of consistently increasing dividends, a great balance sheet, high margins, plenty of competitive advantages (such as scale, barriers to entry, and IP), and a clear runway for plenty of forward-looking growth.

I want a business that I can easily understand (one within my circle of competence). The risks can't be too great. And then I want to invest when undervaluation is present."

What indicators are deal-breakers for buying a dividend company?

"A dividend cut is almost always a deal breaker. A static dividend is also a problem, albeit to a lesser degree. Extreme overvaluation would usually be a deal breaker. A long-term issue with growth in the business or the dividend isn't necessarily a deal breaker, but that would be a red flag. And then an extremely low yield is usually a problem insofar as it would take way too many years and way too much growth to make sense of the investment from an income standpoint. I rarely buy a stock with a yield below 1%. And anything below 0.5% is almost automatically excluded for me."

◆ ◆ ◆

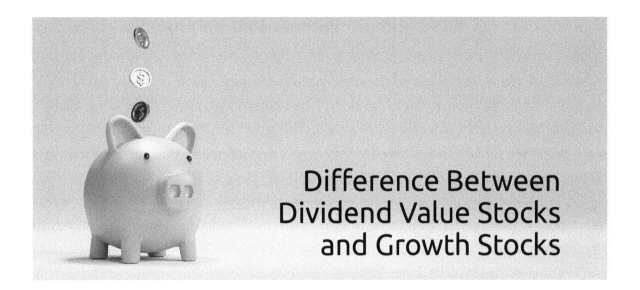

Difference Between Dividend Value Stocks and Growth Stocks

D*ividend stocks are more categorized as value stocks.* Growth stocks are those companies that are considered to have the potential to outperform the overall market over time because of their future potential. Value stocks are classified as companies that are currently trading below what they are really worth and will thus provide a superior return.

The difference between dividend stocks and growth stocks is based on how you emphasize each asset's return, and how the company behind each stock plans for long-term growth. With a dividend stock, you're looking to make money off steady dividend payments over time. With a growth stock, you're looking to make money from a price increase and subsequent capital gains.

Growth stocks generally do not pay dividends but reinvest all earnings back into the company for growth and give nothing to their shareholders. Over the long run, companies that pay dividends have outperformed growth companies that don't offer a regular shareholder dividend payout.

The most important difference between non dividend paying growth stocks and dividend stocks is that dividend-paying stocks allow you to relax during downturns in the market because they provide you a continued increasing source of income to live on if you need the money.

During significant downturns, many growth stocks do not provide any income. If you are retired and do not have other sources of income, you might have to sell your shares at a significant loss just to survive and live. This could dramatically reduce your total retirement portfolio and compromise your lifestyle for the rest of your life.

Another added advantage to dividend-paying stocks is when they cut dividend, it warns you that the company is in trouble. When companies cut dividends, it is recommended that you sell the stock the next day. This gives you time to get out before the stock drops too far in value. There are very few early warnings with growth stocks that do not pay dividends.

Growth companies like Netflix, that do not pay a dividend, dropped 74% without warning over a 5-month period beginning in November 2021. Dividend companies may drop significantly in price, but, as long as they do not cut dividends, you can feel comfortable keeping that company. Check out how the dividend achievers and aristocrats did during the 2008 to 2009 recession.

The best dividend stocks are those that have paid and hopefully have increased dividends every year consistently for more than 25 years. These companies have stood the test of time and should continue to be around for a long time. From the year 2000 through 2021, these dividend-paying companies experienced three major bear markets where the S&P 500 dropped between 32% and 54%. Even during these times, they continued to increase or maintain their dividends, which is an indication of very safe, stable, and strong companies.

Many growth stocks have not been around very long, nor have they proven themselves over time. Growth stocks have greater risk and can default without warning—especially in times of great turmoil. Does anyone remember Enron or Worldcom?

Investors in growth stocks want to see a price increase faster over time because all profits are put back into the company and not paid to the stockholders. This allows the company to grow faster and give you more equity value. What they don't realize is that many dividend companies can also grow exponentially over time and still give the owner passive income for their life. These are examples of dividend growth stocks: McDonald's (MCD), Texas Instruments (TXN), and Whirlpool (WHR).

Other blue-chip companies may be undervalued for a couple of years before they move upward. During this time, you are getting high dividend returns, which you use to buy more shares. Reinvestment in shares can double or triple the equity value and growth even though the share prices go up slowly. Reinvestment of your dividends is like a rocket booster that can propel you to new heights of wealth. Reinvest as much of your dividends as you can.

Taking advantage of market drops

It is very important to take advantage of big drops in the market and buy these dividend paying stocks when they are on sale (undervalued). Fortunately, the dividends you receive allow you the extra cash to buy when the market is down. Over time, you will see an increase in the equity growth of those companies.

In market downturns, the income you receive from dividends will be consistent and usually continue to grow over time because it is based on the number of shares of that company you have. During a bear market, many blue-chip dividend-paying companies increase dividend payouts quarterly to keep their loyal shareholders. Those with dividend stocks may even look forward to downturns in the market because they have a constant source of increasing income to live and extra money to buy more stocks on sale.

Nathan Winklepleck writes in his book ***Dividend Growth Machine: How to Build a Worry-Free Retirement with Dividend Stocks*** (Dividend Investing) (pp. 83–84). Kindle Edition.

"As a dividend investor, you would prefer that the stock market go down in value. Not up. Let me explain. We went through an example with Coca-Cola's stock staying at $40. Now let's assume its stock falls to $20 immediately after you buy it. And the stock price never recovers. Not even after 20 years. Can you imagine the chaos this would cause on Wall Street? Account values halved with no hope for any positive returns? But you? You'd be jumping for joy. Here's why.

In year #1, you still receive your $33 in dividend income like you did in our previous example. Always remember, dividend income and stock prices are not linked. The stock price falling to $20 doesn't mean the dividend goes away.

When the stock price was $40, your $33 of dividend income purchased an extra 0.83 shares. With the price now at $20, your dividend re-investment buys twice as many shares—an extra 1.65 shares after year #1.

In the 2nd year, your dividend income would be $37.31. If the stock stays at $20, that's good for another 1.86 shares. The lower the price, the more shares you can buy. Simple, right? So, if the price stays at $20—you're going to get rich real quick.

When Coca-Cola's stock price stayed at $40, you were able to accumulate 73.6 shares over 20 years. With the stock price at $20 for the entire period, you would be able to build up an astounding 244 shares!

That nets you $4,381 in total dividend income. In Year # 20 alone, you received $812—an 81% return on your initial investment in a single year! That's not even the best part. The value of your shares at the end of year #20 is higher at $20 per share than it would be if the stock had remained at $40. Your Coca-Cola stock would be worth $4,069—quadruple your initial investment! The dividend strategy is so robust that you quadruple your money even though stock prices fell by 50%."

Lack of growth does not mean these stocks don't perform well. Dividend-paying stocks become a safe haven during both bull and bear markets. They tend to fall less than their non-dividend-paying counterparts. The presence of a dividend acts as an assurance that things aren't as bad with these companies as they could potentially be with others.

There is a clear relationship between dividend growth and the price of the stock. As the dividends increase each year, it forces the price of the stock price to increase.

JP Morgan Asset Management (JPMAM) conducted a study in 2013 that looked at U.S. dividend-paying stocks' investment performance versus those that don't pay dividends (U.S. dividends for the long term, 2013). The study tracked companies from 1972 to 2010 (38 years) through all the ups and downs during that time.

JPMAM found that companies that paid and raised their dividend payouts returned an average of 9.5% per year over this period. In contrast, non-dividend-paying companies returned just 1.6% over the same time. We must point out that increasing dividend payments was a large factor in the 9.5% yearly performance. An increasing dividend means company profits were probably growing over this period.

When you reinvest the dividends back into your dividend paying company, it becomes a growth stock. Going back to 1960 (1960–2021), 84% of the total return of the S&P 500 Index can be attributed to reinvested dividends, according to a recent study by Hartford Funds.

◆　◆　◆

Dividends and Taxes

nvestors must pay taxes on their dividends, but how much they pay depends on their income and whether the dividends are qualified or ordinary. Some realty companies (REITs) that pay dividends are non-qualified, such as Getty Realty (GTY), and you pay your standard tax rate. All other companies listed later in this book pay qualified dividends.

Qualified dividends receive more favorable tax treatment but must meet a few criteria. They must be issued by a U.S. corporation that is publicly traded on major exchanges and indices, such as S&P 500, Dow Jones, or NASDAQ. Most dividends from U.S. companies are qualified but only if you own the stock for more than 60 days during the 121-day period that begins 60 days before the ex-dividend date.

The ex-dividend date, otherwise called the ex-date, typically comes one or two business days ahead of the record date. The record date is the day on which the company checks its records to identify shareholders of the company. An investor must be listed on that date to be eligible for a dividend payout that quarter. **Therefore, to be eligible for dividends, you must buy or own the stock at least one business day before the ex-dividend date**.

The dividend payout date, also known as the pay or payable date, is the day on which a declared stock dividend is scheduled to be paid (mailed out) to eligible investors. This date can be up to a month after the ex-dividend date.

- To find these key dates for your individual companies, go to your Schwab account and click on the stock symbol.

♦ To verify that you received your dividends, go to your Schwab account, and click "history" up on top. This will show you all your account transactions, including dividend payouts.

The tax rates for ordinary (non-qualified) dividends (typically those that are paid out from most common or preferred stocks) are the same rates as you pay on regular income, such as salary or wages. This ranges somewhere between 10% and 37% for the 2023 tax year, depending on your income. Income tax and capital gains rates change over time, but in recent years, capital gains rates have been substantially lower.

Currently, the 2023 tax schedule for qualified dividends features only three levels:

♦ **Those who earn less than a sum of $44,625 annually** or are in the 10% and 12% tax brackets pay no taxes on the dividend income. If your income is below $89,250 for a married couple filing jointly, you will probably not owe any taxes on your dividend income.

♦ **Single taxpayers earning more than $44,265 up to $492,300 and married couples filing jointly who earn from $89,250 up to $553,850** are in the 22%, 24%, and 32% tax brackets, and must pay their taxes on dividends at a 15% tax rate.

♦ **Individuals earning $492,300 or more, and married couples earning more than $553,850** are in the 35% or 37% tax bracket and pay only 20% of their annual dividend income in taxes. When the taxes are paid, you will get a step-up basis by Schwab on those stocks where you reinvested your dividends.

♦ Learn more about current tax rates: https://www.nerdwallet.com/article/taxes /dividend-tax-rate

In addition to potentially paying the dividend taxes described above, dividend investors with modified adjusted gross incomes above $200,000 (for single taxpayers) or $250,000 (for married couples filing jointly) are also potentially subject to paying the Net Investment Income Tax.

This tax is assessed regardless of whether the dividends received are classified as qualified or ordinary. The Net Investment Income Tax is an additional 3.8% tax that applies to dividend income (as well as realized gains) and increases the effective total tax rate on dividends and other investment income.

Yet, even with this surcharge, qualified dividends are taxed at significantly better rates versus regular income. That doesn't reduce the risk of investing in the stock, but it does offer the prospect of keeping more of your hard-earned gains for yourself.

When you are buying dividend stocks in your tax-deferred account, such as a 401K, IRA, or Roth IRA, you do not pay taxes on your reinvested dividend income that year. Instead, you will pay taxes on your compounded gains once you start to withdraw money in your retirement. The great exception to this is if you are in a Roth IRA. Unlike a 401K or IRA, where your cash deposits into the account are made with pre-tax dollars, all your cash deposits into a Roth IRA account are made with after-tax dollars, and so you never pay income tax on withdrawals or gains made in the future.

Every year in February, Charles Schwab will send you a document called a "1099." They will also send a copy to the IRS. This 1099 will tell you how much dividend income you collected in the previous year, so that you can calculate your taxes on it. Again, be sure to consult with a tax professional (which I am not).

Dividend yield

The dividend yield is a stock's annual dividend payment as a percentage of the stock price per share. If a share costs $100 and pays $3 in dividends each year, you will get a dividend yield of 3% each year. Keep in mind that the value of your money decreases every year due to effects of inflation, which averages about 2.7%. In July 2022, the inflation rate was above 9%, the highest in 40 years. Dividend investing is the safest and best way to keep up with or beat inflation today.

The Coca-Cola company symbol KO has consistently paid and increased dividends every year for the past 61 years. Today, late 2022, Coke is at $65/share with an annual dividend of $1.76, resulting in a dividend yield of 2.7% ($1.76 dividend/$65 share price). **But if you were wise enough to pick up some shares of Coke at $22.00 during the 2008 crisis, the dividend yield on your investment this year would be ($1.68/$22) or nearly 8%.**

In 1988 and 1989, Warren Buffett bought shares of Coke at a split-adjusted average price of just $2.45. He owns 400 million shares of Coke and has made 2,571% in the process, combined with more than $9 billion he has received from Coke in dividend payments. Today, Buffett's dividend yield is 71.8% on his original purchase price. As one of the richest men in the world, he still pays only 23.8% taxes on his dividend income.

Given enough time, any of us can achieve a dividend yield that replace our income. The sooner you get started, the larger your nest egg will be. It is a very simple way to build extreme wealth, and this path is open to anyone with some foresight and a little discipline.

◆ ◆ ◆

The Key to Successful Investing Is Focusing on the Right Numbers

Most investors (speculators) have great joy as the price of the stock goes up but feel great anxiety and frustration as the stock price goes down. Price is the wrong investment number. The three most important investment numbers are:

- The monthly passive cash income you receive from dividends.

- The average annual dividend growth.

- The dividend yield on your original investment.

- The stock's total return with dividends reinvested.

The most important number of the three is average annual dividend growth.

One example of a great aristocrat dividend stock is Abbvie (ABBV). This company demonstrates the importance and value of increasing dividends every year. In 2013, when a share of stock was $34, the dividend was 4.71%. Over the next 8 years, the value of your stock grew to $175 per share and now is at $165. More importantly, in 2022, you will get a 16.59% in dividend returns on the original shares you bought in 2013. This is greater than 3.5 times your original dividend yield. **This is a very important concept and key to obtaining long-term passive income for life!**

Stock price has no effect on your dividend or dividend growth. Even if the price of your stocks drop in half, your dividend income will usually continue to increase every year. Almost all of the blue-chip companies listed later have continued to increase their dividend amount each year, even in down markets. Growth of the dividends tend to increase the price of the stock over time.

Abbvie (ABBV) $34/share in 2013 and $153/share 2022 (8 year range $34 to $175) Div paid since 1926 - 50										
Health Care- 8 year Dividend growth rate (DGR10) 325% / Yield 3.6%										
Average Dividend growh rate for: 3 year - 13.2% / 5 year - 18.4%										
Year	2013	2014	2015	2016	2017	2018	2019	2020	2021	2022
Dividend	$1.60	$1.75	$2.10	$2.35	$2.63	$3.95	$4.39	$4.84	$5.31	$5.64
100 shares	$160	$175	$210	$235	$263	$395	$439	$484	$531	$564
1000 shares	$1,600	$1,750	$2,100	$2,350	$2,630	$3,950	$4,390	$4,840	$5,310	$5,640
Dividend %	4.71%	5.15%	6.18%	6.91%	7.74%	11.62%	12.91%	14.24%	15.62%	16.59%

When you understand the value and the power of income return from dividends, you may want to sell off some of your mutual funds or growth companies and buy undervalued dividend paying blue-chip stocks.

Dividend Kings

Here are examples of Dividend Kings. Each Dividend King has a 50-year track record of increasing dividend payouts each year.

Lowe's (LOW)

Lowe's (LOW) has paid dividends since 1921 and has increased them every year for 61 years. Note that the dividends increased each year as did the dividend percentages paid on the original investment. Pay attention to the increased return on your dividends. Lowe's average 16% dividend growth has allowed the dividend to double every 4.5 years, and now you are getting a 15% dividend return each year on your original investment.

Lowe's (LOW) $28/share in 2010 and $215/share in 2022 (11 year range $28 to $260) Div paid since 1961 - 61 years Div inc												
Consumer Discretionary 11 year dividend growth rate (DGR11) 1050% / Yield 2%												
Average Dividend growth: current - 31% / 3 year - 16.5% / 5 year - 17.4% / 10 year - 18.9% / 20 year - 25%												
Year	2010	2011	2012	2013	2014	2015	2016	2017	2018	2019	2020	2021	2022
Dividend	$0.40	$0.53	$0.62	$0.70	$0.87	$1.07	$1.33	$1.58	$1.85	$2.13	$2.30	$3.20	$4.20
100 shares	$40	$53	$62	$70	$87	$107	$133	$158	$185	$213	$230	$320	$420
1000 shares	$400	$530	$620	$700	$870	$1,070	$1,330	$1,580	$1,850	$2,130	$2,300	$3,200	$4,200
Dividend %	1.43%	1.89%	2.21%	2.50%	3.11%	3.82%	4.75%	5.64%	6.61%	7.61%	8.21%	11.43%	15.00%

Texas Instruments (TXN)

Dividend investing is the perfect investment for retirees or those who are planning to retire. Nathan Winklepleck's YouTube video demonstrates the power of dividend growth for those who want to retire comfortably. Here is a summary of what he says in the video, using Texas Instruments as an example.

- ◆ Nathan Winklepleck video: https://www.youtube.com/watch?v=luWaRka9L0Y

Let's take a hypothetical case where you retired at the worst possible time, December 31, 2007. The S&P 500 was at its all-time high and then began the great financial crisis, where both the S&P 500 and Texas Instruments dropped by more than 50 percent. Your initial investment of $1,000,000 in December 2007 would have bought 29,940 shares of Texas Instruments (TXN) at $33 a share. In 2008, the share price of Texas Instruments dropped to $16 per share resulting in a **value drop of your portfolio from $1,000,000 to only $464,671**. (The market may have caused the price to drop in half, but this does not represent the true value of the company.)

In 2008, you would have received a dividend of $0.40 per share, resulting in **dividend income of $11,976**. In 2009, the dividend went from $0.40 to $0.44, increasing your income by 10%. In 2010, your dividend income increased another 10% and again in 2011. If each year you spent all the dividends, in 2021 your yearly dividend would have increased by 10 times, giving you a dividend income of **$122,000 that year. If you would have reinvested the dividends, your dividend income would have been more than $167,000 a year.**

The market value of those shares also increased from $16 a share to $188 a share in **2021.** This means your 29,940 shares would have been worth **more than 5.6 million dollars. If you reinvested those dividends, your portfolio would have been worth more than $8,000,000.**

The lowest dividend growth rate per year with Texas Instruments was 8.3%. If we use that going forward for the next 10 years to 2031, you would be receiving $306,000. More importantly, during those past years, you did not add to your portfolio or reinvest the dividends but spent all of your dividend income on personal living expenses.

If you fast forward to **2032** (again, assuming you still own the same 29,940 shares and assuming the dividend yield is the highest it's been), the estimated value of the portfolio would be **more than 9.4 million dollars.** Again, remember, that's even with you spending all of this money each and every year and you never reinvested any of these dividends back into the stock.

Texas Instruments (TXN) $25/share in 2010 and $178/share 2022 (11 year range $25 to $202) Div paid since 1962 - 19 years Div inc												
Information Technology - 10 year dividend growth rate (DGR10) 938% / Yield 2.76%												
Average Dividend growh rate for: 3 year - 17% / 5 year - 20.9% / 10 year - 23.2% / 20 year - 23.9%												
Year	2010	2011	2012	2013	2014	2015	2016	2017	2018	2019	2020	2021	2022
Dividend	$0.49	$0.56	$0.72	$1.07	$1.24	$1.40	$1.64	$2.12	$2.63	$3.21	$3.72	$4.21	$4.60
100 shares	$49	$56	$72	$107	$124	$140	$164	$212	$263	$321	$372	$421	$460
1000 shares	$490	$560	$720	$1,070	$1,240	$1,400	$1,640	$2,120	$2,630	$3,210	$3,720	$4,210	$4,600
Dividend %	1.96%	2.24%	2.88%	4.28%	4.96%	5.60%	6.56%	8.48%	10.52%	12.84%	14.88%	16.84%	18.40%

In 2022, Texas Instruments is paying dividend income return of 18.4% on the original shares bought in 2010. These payment increases should increase every year with those companies that increase their dividends every year. Texas Instruments is one of the great companies that demonstrates both incredible dividend growth and equity growth. In the chart above you can see that the $49 dividend in 2010 doubled by 2013 and quadrupled in just seven years in 2017. **Over 11 years, the money you received in dividends has now grown to almost 10 times the $49 in 2010 to $460 in 2022.** This is because of their average 23% annual dividend growth over that time. This is why dividend growth is the most important criterion in selecting dividend paying stocks.

High-quality and well-diversified portfolio

By building a well-diversified portfolio of high-quality businesses that has a ton of free cash flow AND can afford to both pay a dividend today and increase that dividend over time, you will never worry about retirement. This type of dividend portfolio will offer you many advantages:

1. You're going to have consistent income that you can spend today.

2. That income is going to grow for you each and every year throughout your retirement, likely increasing above and beyond inflation.

3. You're likely to increase the market value of your portfolio over time.

4. You're going to give yourself a reason to continue owning your stocks even when the market value is declining.

Over your lifetime, you will see the market go down by 10, 20, 30, 40, or even 50 percent. If you have a well-diversified portfolio of dividend growth stocks, you can continue to receive a continual source of increasing dividend income. You're not going to need to sell any shares at bad prices just to fund your expenses. You will sleep a lot better at night knowing that you own some of the world's best companies and that those companies are paying you a cash dividend each and every quarter, regardless of what happens to stock prices.

With dividend investing, you will no longer worry about the 4% rule. This is a rule of thumb that suggests retirees can safely withdraw the amount equal to 4 percent of their savings during the year they retire and then adjust for inflation each subsequent year for 30 years. With the dividend investing strategy you never need to sell any of your portfolio because you are living on the dividends. Your stock portfolio now becomes generational wealth.

Individual dividend stocks vs. dividend ETF (exchange-traded funds)

If you are afraid to buy individual stocks, you can buy the Schwab U.S. dividend equity ETF fund (SCHD). It contains 100 well-diversified dividend-paying companies (stocks). From January 3, 2022, to December 4, 2022, the S&P 500 dropped -14.6% compared to a drop of only -2.3% in the SCHD ETF. This demonstrates how dividend stocks resist dramatic drops in the market. SCHD has an expense ratio of only 0.06% with an annual dividend yield of 3.44%. **A similar portfolio made up of 25 individual dividend stocks listed in the next chapter increased by +6% during the same time period.**

- Schwab US dividend equity fund research on Morningstar:
  https://www.morningstar.com/etfs/arcx/schd/portfolio

- Nathan Winklepleck's dividend ETF video:
  https://www.youtube.com/watch?v=64NEiyoNBIM

- Dave Van Knapp's dividend ETF video:
  https://www.youtube.com/watch?v=gY6dpRXSBQs

The great news with dividend investing is that you will hardly ever have to sell any of your stocks. Warren Buffett is fond of saying: "The best time to sell a stock is . . . never."

There's only one situation when you should sell a dividend stock, and that is when they cut their dividend. Sell it the same or next day, using a market order. If a dividend blue-chip cannot pay its dividend, it means one of two things:

- The management is no longer very shareholder-friendly, in which case you want out.

- The business has deteriorated to the point that it is no longer able to pay the dividend that it once was. In which case you want out.

When you are investing with Schwab, you can set up a dividend alert that announces the amount of the upcoming dividend, the dividend ex-date and dividend payout date for each one of your dividend-paying stocks. This will tell you if the company is raising dividends, keeping them the same, cutting or eliminating dividends.

Remember, one of the greatest advantages of dividend stocks is that they give you an early warning when the company may be in trouble. This is not true with pure growth stocks or some dividend-paying bank stocks.

◆　◆　◆

Guidelines for Buying the Best Dividend-Paying Stocks

T*here are currently more than 12,000 stocks* available for purchase on U.S. stock exchanges.

Achievers, Aristocrats, and Kings

- Of those, only 2,000-plus currently pay a dividend (16.8%).

- Just 347 (2.9%) have paid and increased their dividends for the past 10 years. These are called dividend achievers.

- In this group, there are 65 (0.5%) companies that have consistently increased their dividends for more than 25 years. These are called Dividend Aristocrats.

- Dividend Kings are 46 companies that have increased their dividend for more than 50 years. These are the bluest of the blue-chip stocks and have stood the test of time.

The reason we choose to buy dividend paying stocks is because they outperform non-dividend-paying stocks for three reasons:

1. A company that pays dividends is likely to be generating earnings or cash flows so that it can pay dividends to shareholders. This excludes "pre-earnings" start-ups and failing businesses. In short, it excludes the riskiest stocks.

2. A business that pays consistent dividends must be more selective with the growth projects it takes on because a portion of its cash flows are being paid out as dividends. Scrutinizing over capital allocation decisions likely adds to shareholder value.

3. Stocks that pay dividends are willing to reward shareholders with cash payments. This is a sign that management is shareholder friendly.

Dividend aristocrats have historically seen smaller drawdowns during recessions versus the S&P 500. This makes holding through recessions that much easier. Case in point: In 2008, the Dividend Aristocrats Index declined 22%. That same year, the S&P 500 declined 49%.

Great businesses with strong competitive advantages tend to be able to generate stronger cash flows during recessions. This allows them to gain market share while weaker businesses fight to stay alive. The Dividend Aristocrats Index has beaten the market over the last 28 years.

Instead of owning 66 stocks, you will probably do well owning just 15 to 25 dividend aristocrats that are diversified over 6 to 8 different sectors. Diversification is simply keeping your eggs in lots of different baskets. If one or two stocks drop, you still have 20 stocks that are plugging away and continuing to pay you dividends. You will almost never need to sell your shares of Dividend Aristocrats.

- Simply Safe Dividends list of dividend achievers:
  https://www.simplysafedividends.com/world-of-dividends/posts/43-dividend-achievers

- Simply Safe Dividends list of dividend aristocrats:
  https://www.simplysafedividends.com/world-of-dividends/posts/6-dividend
  -aristocrats-list

- Simply Safe Dividends list of dividend kings:
  https://www.simplysafedividends.com/world-of-dividends/posts/41-dividend-kings

Dividend Kings have withstood periods of inflation, recessions, market crashes, political instability, changing customer trends, and critical technology advancements for more than 50 years. Lowe's (LOW), Procter & Gamble (PG), Coca-Cola (KO), and 3M Company (MMM) are examples of Dividend Kings. All Dividend Kings have stood the test of time and have proven themselves successful over many years. Coca-Cola (KO) has been around for more than 120 years.

Your intent is to always keep these companies in your portfolio and not sell them. The only time you would sell them is when they cut or stop paying dividends.

Remember, your main focus needs to be on the dividend growth and your increasing dividend income, and secondarily on dividend yield.

Dividend growth rate

Dividend growth rate is the annualized percentage rate of growth that a particular stock's dividend undergoes over a period of time. A history of strong dividend growth could mean future dividend growth is likely, which can signal long-term profitability. This number is probably the most important indicator of long-term return in your portfolio. You want the average dividend growth to be higher than the inflation rate. Select a 3-year and 5-year annualized growth rate greater than 5% or higher.

The price of the stock usually goes up as the dividend goes up. The price of the stock will go up faster with an average annual dividend growth of 10%, compared to a stock with an average dividend growth of only 2%. As an example, Lowe's (LOW) had an average annual growth of 18.9% over the past 10 years with a significant increase in the equity value.

Lowe's (LOW) $28/share in 2010 and $215/share in 2022 (11 year range $28 to $260) Div paid since 1961 - 61 years Div inc												
Consumer Discretionary 11 year dividend growth rate (DGR11) 1050% / Yield 2%												
Average Dividend growth: current - 31% / 3 year - 16.5% / 5 year - 17.4% / 10 year - 18.9% / 20 year - 25%												
Year	2010	2011	2012	2013	2014	2015	2016	2017	2018	2019	2020	2021	2022
Dividend	$0.40	$0.53	$0.62	$0.70	$0.87	$1.07	$1.33	$1.58	$1.85	$2.13	$2.30	$3.20	$4.20
100 shares	$40	$53	$62	$70	$87	$107	$133	$158	$185	$213	$230	$320	$420
1000 shares	$400	$530	$620	$700	$870	$1,070	$1,330	$1,580	$1,850	$2,130	$2,300	$3,200	$4,200
Dividend %	1.43%	1.89%	2.21%	2.50%	3.11%	3.82%	4.75%	5.64%	6.61%	7.61%	8.21%	11.43%	15.00%

- Lowe's average dividend growth rate:
  https://www.digrin.com/stocks/detail/LOW/

Compare this to Northwest Natural (NWN) with an average 10-year dividend growth of only 1.5%. Northwest Natural (NWN) is another Dividend King that has increased their dividends every year for 66 years, but the dividend increase has been only 0.5% a year, even though they give a dividend yield of 4.2%.

Northwest Natural (NWN) $44/share in 2010 and $54/share 2022 (11 year range $44 to $75) 66 years Div inc												
Utility- 10 year dividend-growth rate (DGR10) 108% / Yield 3.6%												
Average Dividend growth: current - 0.5% / 3 year - 0.5% / 5 year - 0.5% / 10 year - 1.5% / 20 year - 2.5%												
Year	2010	2011	2012	2013	2014	2015	2016	2017	2018	2019	2020	2021	2022
Dividend	$1.74	$1.76	$1.78	$1.79	$1.85	$1.86	$1.87	$1.88	$1.89	$1.90	$1.91	$1.92	$1.93
100 shares	$174	$176	$178	$179	$185	$186	$187	$188	$189	$190	$191	$192	$193
1000 shares	$1,740	$1,760	$1,780	$1,790	$1,850	$1,860	$1,870	$1,880	$1,890	$1,900	$1,910	$1,920	$1,930
Dividend %	3.95%	4.00%	4.05%	4.07%	4.20%	4.23%	4.25%	4.27%	4.30%	4.32%	4.34%	4.36%	4.39%

- Northwest Natural average dividend growth rate:
  https://www.digrin.com/stocks/detail/NWN/

Lowe's share price grew from $28 a share to $192 (686% increase) in the 11 years compared to Northwest Natural that grew from only $44 per share to $47 per share (7% increase) during the same time frame. This demonstrates the importance of high dividend growth to both your personal dividend income as well as equity growth of the company.

Lowe's (LOW) has increased their dividends for 61 years and has a dividend yield of 2.19% with a high dividend annualized growth rate (dividend increase) currently of 31% and over 16% over the last 3-year, 5-year, 10-year, and 20-year.

After 11 years, your dividend on 100 shares at Lowe's (LOW), grew your dividend income from $40 to $420 (1050% increase) compared to your 100 shares with Northwest Natural (NWN) that only grew from $174 to $193 (11% increase). I would rather have a stock that pays a 2.19% dividend with a 16% dividend increase each year, compared to a stock that has a 4.2% dividend stock with only a 0.5% increase each year.

Avoiding high dividend yield traps

When investing in dividend paying assets, people often confuse high yields with good investment opportunities. Stocks and funds that pay high yields like 8% and above but don't offer any prospect of capital gains are referred to as yield traps. A high dividend yield usually indicates a low-quality, high-risk company. Most stocks with yields of 6% and higher are being priced for a dividend cut. At minimum, they are being priced for low future dividend growth.

A stock with a 2% dividend yield and 10% average yearly dividend growth will ultimately produce more dividend income than a stock with a 6% dividend yield and

0.5% dividend growth. And quite a bit more than a 10%-yielding stock that (eventually) must cut their dividend. Don't fall in love with yield. You want sustainable, low-risk, predictable dividend growth for many years to come. Don't get too greedy for dividends now.

Annual percentage of dividend returns are more important than dividend yield

The dividend yield is a stock's annual dividend payment as a percentage of the stock price per share. Most dividend investors look for a yield somewhere between 2.5%, to 6%. But remember, the most important number is dividend growth and the average annual return with dividends reinvested. Over half of the funds listed in this book are below 2.5% but they have very high annual dividend-growth rate and high annual returns.

Using a stock return calculator and average dividend return (ADR) calculator which automatically factors and calculates dividend reinvestment (DRIP).

https://dqydj.com/stock-return-calculator/

Remember, "past performance is no guarantee of future results"!

You will notice in the chart below that the highest annual return percentage and dollar return came from those companies that had lower dividend yields with high 10-year average dividend growth rates. Compare these companies with those on the bottom that have high dividend yield and low dividend growth rates. The average annual return on these companies (IBM, WBA, and LEG) over the past ten years is only 1/10th the return of some of the lower dividend yield companies.

United Health (UNH) dividend yield is 1.33% with a 10-year average dividend growth rate of 25.6% and an annual 10-year return of 27.8%. A onetime initial $10,000 investment grew to over $116,000 compared to IBM which returned only $11,000 during that 10-year time frame with dividends automatically reinvested.

It is important to keep these high returning companies on your watch list and take advantage of them when they become undervalued. As in March 2020 when the S&P 500 dropped 37% it would have been a great time to sell some of these higher dividend yielding companies with low returns and trade them in for these higher annual percentage return companies. United Health (UNH) price dropped more than half in March 2009.

You will also note that most of these dividend growth companies have given higher average annual returns then the S&P 500 or Warren Buffet's Berkshire Hathaway company.

Ticker Symbol	Company	Sector	Cur Price	Dividend Yield	Dividend	Payout Ratio	10Y ADGR	Annual %return 2013 to 2023	$10k Return 2013 to 2023
UNH	United Health	HC	500	1.32%	$6.60	29%	25.6%	27.8%	116k
NOC	Northrop Grumman	I	471	1.47%	$6.92	26%	12.1%	25.2%	95k
LMT	Lockheed Martin	I	463	2.59%	$12.00	42%	12.6%	21.5%	69k
TXN	Texas Instruments	IT	175	2.83%	$4.96	48%	22.4%	21.1%	67k
LOW	Lowe's	CD	213	1.97%	$4.20	28%	18.9%	21.0%	67k
AMP	Ameriprise	F	351	1.42%	$5.00	21%	18.8%	19.8%	60k
SBUX	Starbucks	CS	107	1.98%	$2.12	68%	20.9%	16.0%	43k
AOS	A. O. Smith	I	67.2	1.79%	$1.20	36%	21.6%	15.2%	41k
BRK B	Berkshire Hathaway		308	0.00%	$0.00	NA	NA	12.7%	33k
SPY	S&P 500	ETF	407	1.55%	$6.32	NA	7.4%	12.3%	32k
LEG	Leggett & Platt	CD	34.6	5.09%	$1.76	65%	4.2%	5.1%	16k
WBA	Walgreens Boots	CS	36.8	5.22%	$1.92	42%	7.3%	2.7%	13k
IBM	IBM	IT	135	4.89%	$6.60	72%	9.5%	1.2%	11k
	Source: https://dqydj.com/stock-return-calculator/								

Which stocks to buy now

Every one of these stocks on the list has met stringent requirements to make the list, and any one would be a good choice, but the most important step is to buy them when they are **undervalued**. This is why the list is sorted by the 52-week range (52w). Focus on those companies that are at their 52-week low or up to 40% of their low.

The next column to look at is the IQT newsletter undervalue price. If the current price is below the IQT newsletter price, then it is considered a good buying opportunity. There are two other columns to look at to determine if this stock is undervalued. One of them is the Morningstar value rating. A 5 rating is severely undervalued, and a 4 would be undervalued. The last rating is the Simply Safe dividend rating, which can be a U for undervalue, R for reasonably priced, and an O for overvalued.

These four columns will help select companies that are undervalued at the time of the publishing of the Dr. Ace Freedom Fund list. Go to www.doctorace.com/dividendlinks/ to obtain the most updated list.

Great dividend companies have stood the test of time and will almost always rebound. The only time you sell is when they cut or stop paying dividends. Dividend yields can be higher in bear markets, when stock prices have fallen dramatically. During deep market downturns of 25% to 50%, you can buy companies that normally pay dividends at a discount of 1% to 2% and lock in incredible dividend yields of 3% to 5% with these companies.

The Ace List

Below are examples of great dividend companies as of April 2023. These are taken from the list of dividend achievers, aristocrats, and kings. 90% of these companies have been recommended by the Investment Quality Trends (IQT) newsletter. One requirement for being on this list is that none of these companies cut their dividends during the last recession. I have also chosen not to have any MLPs (Master Limited Partnerships) or REIT (Real Estate Investment Trust) on this list because their dividends are non-qualified.

We are looking for the most undervalued stocks that meet our requirements. This list is sorted by the lowest to highest 52-week price range with the highest dividend yield.

This list of stocks is for educational purposes only, not investment, legal, or tax advice. It is not a recommendation or offer to buy or sell any security. Past performance is no guarantee of future results. Although all figures are thought to be correct, no guarantee is expressed, nor should any be implied. Do your own research, and invest at your own risk!

Ticker Symbol	Company	Sector	52w	One year return	IQT Under Value Price	Cur Price	Dividend Yield	Dividend	Payout Ratio	Cur Div GR	5Y ADGR	10Y ADGR	20Y ADGR	Annual %return 2013 to 2023	P/E <20	Years of Div incr	S&P	Div Safe	MS value 5 is best	SSD VR	Since
FLIC	First Long Island	F	0	-30.6%	NR	13.5	6.22%	$0.84	40%	5.0%	9%	10.3%	10.0%	7.5%	9	28	B+	70	3	U	1927
HRL	Hormel Foods	CS	1	-22.6%	41	39.9	2.76%	$1.10	59%	5.8%	8.9%	13.2%	13.0%	12.7%	25	57	A+	99	3	U	1891
JNJ	Johnson&Johnson	HC	1	-12.5%	119	155	2.92%	$4.52	44%	6.6%	5.9%	6.4%	9.3%	12.6%	17	60	A-	99	3	U	1886
LHX	L3 Harris	I	1	-21.0%	149	196	2.33%	$4.56	35%	9.8%	14.0%	12.8%	20.0%	18.3%	17	19	A-	80	4	U	1895
MMM	3 M Corp	I	1	-29.4%	200	105	5.71%	$6.00	59%	0.7%	5.9%	10.4%	8.0%	6.0%	12	63	A	60	4	U	1902
OZK	Bank OZK	F	1	-19.9%	27	34.2	3.98%	$1.36	28%	11.0%	12.5%	20.4%	20.0%	11.8%	8	25	A	50	4	U	1903
SRCE	1st Source	F	1	-6.7%	43	43.2	2.96%	$1.28	26%	3.2%	10.9%	7.6%	7.0%	13.0%	11	34	A	96	3	U	1863
TSN	Tyson Foods	CS	1	-33.8%	71	59.3	3.24%	$1.92	28%	4.3%	15.4%	27.7%	13.0%	14.1%	10	10	A	99	5	U	1935
WHR	Whirlpool	CD	1	-23.6%	163	132	5.30%	$7.00	36%	0.0%	6.9%	11.0%	7.5%	5.7%	9	11	B+	70	4	U	1911
MDT	Medtronic	HC	1.5	-27.3%	91	80.6	3.37%	$2.72	51%	7.9%	7.9%	10.0%	13.0%	8.3%	14	44	B+	99	4	U	1949
LEG	Leggett & Platt	CD	2	-8.4%	40	31.9	5.52%	$1.76	77%	4.8%	4.4%	4.2%	6.5%	5.1%	16	50	A-	70	4	U	1883
NSC	Norfolk Southern	I	2	-25.7%	134	212	2.55%	$5.40	37%	14.0%	12.0%	10.5%	15.0%	16.9%	17	5	A-	86	4	U	1980
SWK	Stanley Black Decker	I	2	-42.4%	91	80.7	3.97%	$3.20	70%	1.3%	5.7%	6.2%	6.0%	2.4%	32	54	A	80	3	U	1843
TD	Toronto-DoBank	F	2	-24.6%	58	60	4.58%	$2.75	42%	7.9%	9.0%	6.8%	10.0%	8.7%	10	12	A	80	4	U	1855
UNH	United Health	HC	2	-7.3%	413	473	1.40%	$6.60	29%	14.0%	18.7%	25.6%	39.0%	27.8%	22	12	A+	99	3	R	1977
EMN	Eastman Chemical	M	2.5	-24.7%	90	84.3	3.75%	$3.16	39%	3.9%	8.4%	11.1%	6.0%	6.7%	11	12	B+	85	5	U	1920
ENB	Enbridge	E	2.5	-17.2%	57	38.2	6.91%	$2.64	118%	3.2%	11.8%	10.9%	12.0%	9.8%	10	26	B+	70	3	R	1952
RJF	Raymond James	F	2.5	-15.1%	88	93.3	1.80%	$1.68	19%	24.0%	18.3%	14.7%	14.5%	16.9%	11	10	A	99	4	R	1962
UNP	Union Pacific	I	2.5	-26.3%	158	201	2.59%	$5.20	45%	11.0%	13.7%	16.1%	17.2%	15.0%	18	15	A-	88	3	U	1862
ABT	Abbott Lab	HC	3	-14.5%	NR	101	2.04%	$2.04	36%	8.5%	12.0%	10.0%	4.0%	15.0%	24	50	A-	71	3	U	1888
AMGN	Amgen Inc	HC	3	0.0%	237	242	3.52%	$8.52	44%	9.8%	12.0%	28.8%		14.5%	14	10	A-	74	3	U	1980
BKH	Black Hills	U	3	-18.1%	56	53.1	4.71%	$2.50	60%	5.0%	6.4%	4.6%	3.7%	9.6%	19	51	B+	77	4	U	1942
MO	Altria	CS	3	-14.6%	54	44.6	8.43%	$3.76	76%	4.4%	8.4%	8.4%	2.0%	9.5%	9	53	B+	55	4	U	1985
OGE	OGE Energy	U	3	-8.5%	23	35.8	4.64%	$1.66	76%	1.0%	7.0%	7.9%	5.0%	7.4%	16	15	B+	70	3	U	1906
RHI	Robert Half Inter	I	3	-29.5%	80	80.6	2.38%	$1.92	29%	12.0%	11.3%	10.1%		10.5%	14	17	A	96	4	U	1948

Ticker Symbol	Company	Sector	52w	One year return	IQT Under Value Price	Cur Price	Dividend Yield	Dividend	Payout Ratio	Cur Div GR	5Y ADGR	10Y ADGR	20Y ADGR	Annual %return 2013 to 2023	P/E <20	Years of Div incr	S&P	Div Safe	MS value 5 is best	SSD VR	Since
TGT	Target	CD	3	-22.0%	108	166	2.60%	$4.32	66%	20.0%	6.4%	11.1%	14.5%	12.8%	18	50	A-	90	3	R	1902
TROW	T. Rowe Price	F	3	-25.3%	112	113	4.32%	$4.88	60%	1.7%	14.9%	13.3%	14.0%	9.2%	16	35	A	94	3	U	1937
UGI	UGI Corp	U	3	-4.0%	34	34.8	4.14%	$1.44	46%	4.3%	7.7%	7.2%	7.1%	4.2%	12	35	A	99	4	U	1882
WBA	Walgreens Boots	CS	3	-22.8%	53	34.6	5.55%	$1.92	47%	0.5%	4.6%	7.3%	14.7%	2.7%	8	47	B+	79	4	U	1901
WSM	Williams Sonoma	CD	3	-16.1%	89	122	2.95%	$3.60	19%	9.9%	12.0%	14.0%		12.4%	8	12	A	80	5	R	1956
ADP	AutoData Processing	BS	3.5	-2.2%	139	223	2.24%	$5.00	58%	20.0%	12.6%	10.1%	11.9%	19.2%	29	47	A	97	3	U	1949
HD	Home Depot	CD	3.5	-1.4%	283	295	2.83%	$8.36	47%	10.0%	19%	20.3%	20.0%	20.4%	19	14	A+	87	3	U	1978
NOC	Northrop Grumman	I	3.5	3.2%	231	462	1.50%	$6.92	26%	10.0%	12.0%	12.1%	11.0%	25.2%	24	18	A+	80	3	R	1939
THO	Thor Industries	CD	3.5	1.2%	53	79.6	2.26%	$1.80	12%	4.7%	5.4%	11.1%	25.0%	10.0%	10	12	A-	65	4	R	1980
CINF	Cinncinnati Finance	F	4	-17.5%	67	112	2.68%	$3.00	65%	9.5%	6.0%	4.6%	6.0%	13.2%	23	61	B+	71	4	R	1950
COST	Costco	CS	4	-13.7%	277	497	0.72%	$3.60	26%	14.0%	12.0%	12.8%		18.8%	31	18	A	99	3	O	1976
IBM	IBM	IT	4	0.8%	126	131	5.04%	$6.60	72%	0.6%	3.7%	9.5%	13.0%	1.2%	15	26	A-	65	3	R	1911
KR	Kroger	CS	4	-14.0%	40	49.4	2.11%	$1.04	23%	24.0%	12.0%	13.8%		16.1%	11	15	A	71	3	R	1883
BBY	Best Buy	CD	4.5	-13.9%	NR	78.3	4.70%	$3.68	50%	26.0%	20.0%	19.0%		22.9%	12	18	B+	80	4	U	1966
CL	Colgate-Palmolive	CS	4.5	-0.9%	63	75.2	2.55%	$1.92	63%	4.4%	3.0%	4.7%	9.0%	6.4%	26	59	B+	90	3	R	1806
CMCSA	Comcast	C	4.5	-19.0%	41	37.9	3.06%	$1.16	30%	7.4%	13.0%	16.0%		8.2%	10	13	A	89	5	U	1963
GD	General Dynamic	I	4.5	-5.4%	144	228	2.31%	$5.28	41%	5.9%	14.0%	15.3%	11.0%	15.9%	19	30	A+	97	3	R	1899
GS	Goldman Sachs	F	4.5	-0.9%	347	327	3.06%	$10.00	30%	25.0%	20.0%	19.5%	14.0%	12.4%	10	10	A+	60	4	U	1869
HON	Honeywell	I	4.5	-1.8%	118	191	2.16%	$4.12	45%	5.1%	9.0%	10.7%	8.8%	15.2%	24	11	A-	99	4	R	1906
SCHD	Schwab US Div ETF	ETF	4.5	-7.3%	NA	73.2	3.50%	$2.56	NA	11.0%	16.4%	14.8%	NA	13.5%	16	10	NA	NA	5	NA	2011
BEN	Franklin Resources	F	5	-3.5%	NR	27	4.44%	$1.20	38%	3.4%	10.0%	19.1%	13.0%	-1.7%	10	42	A	70	3	R	1947
BRK B	Berkshire Hathaway	ETF	5	-12.5%	NR	309	0.00%	$0.00	NA	NA	NA	NA	NA	12.7%	NA	NA	A	NA	4	NA	1966
PM	Phillip Morris	CS	5	3.5%	85	97.3	5.22%	$5.08	85%	1.6%	3.5%	5.7%		6.8%	18	13	B+	64	3	R	1847
SPY	SPDR S&P500 ETF	ETF	5	-9.4%	NA	409	1.58%	$6.46	NA	9.0%	5.0%	7.4%	7.0%	12.3%	9	13	NA	NA	4	NA	2010
WEC	WEC Energy	U	5	-5.0%	80	94.8	3.29%	$3.12	65%	7.2%	6.0%	10.0%	10.0%	13.2%	21	20	A	87	4	U	1981

Ticker Symbol	Company	Sector	52w	One year return	IQT Under Value Price	Cur Price	Dividend Yield	Dividend	Payout Ratio	Cur Div GR	5Y ADGR	10Y ADGR	20Y ADGR	Annual %return 2013 to 2023	P/E <20	Years of Div incr	S&P	Div Safe	MS value 5 is best	SSD VR	Since
CVX	Chevron	E	5.5	0.2%	NR	163	3.71%	$6.04	30%	6.0%	4.0%	5.7%	7.3%	9.4%	11	34	A-	90	3	O	1879
EPD	Enterprise	E	5.5	0.4%	22	25.9	7.57%	$1.96	76%	2.2%	2.0%	5.9%	6.0%	6.9%	7	23	B+	65	3	R	1968
LOW	Lowe's	CD	5.5	-1.1%	210	200	2.10%	$4.20	29%	31.0%	17.7%	18.9%	24.0%	21.0%	14	61	A+	93	3	U	1921
UNM	Unum Group	F	5.5	25.6%	44	39.6	3.33%	$1.32	21%	10.0%	8.7%	11.5%	4.4%	9.4%	7	13	B+	50	4	O	1848
ABBV	Abbvie	HC	6	-1.7%	132	159	3.72%	$5.92	41%	5.0%	17.7%	11.0%		21.4%	13	50	B+	70	2	O	1926
AFL	Aflac Co	F	6	0.2%	42	64.5	2.60%	$1.68	30%	5.0%	9.7%	8.0%	14.0%	13.5%	14	39	A-	99	4	R	1955
AMP	Ameriprise	F	6	2.0%	135	307	1.63%	$5.00	20%	11.0%	8.7%	18.8%		19.8%	11	16	A-	90	3	O	1894
APD	Air Products	M	6	15.0%	196	287	2.44%	$7.00	62%	8.0%	12.6%	11.4%	11.5%	16.3%	27	40	A	95	4	R	1954
AWR	Am States Water	U	6	-0.2%	78	88.9	1.79%	1.59	60%	8.9%	8.9%	10.0%	6.0%	16.4%	35	67	A	98	3	U	1928
BLK	BlackRock	F	6	-12.4%	574	669	2.99%	$20.00	55%	18.0%	12.6%	11.3%		15.9%	22	12	A	98	3	R	1988
KO	Coca-Cola	CS	6	0.1%	54	62	2.97%	$1.84	71%	4.8%	3.7%	6.0%	8.0%	8.9%	26	59	A+	80	3	R	1886
PG	Procter&Gamble	CS	6	-2.7%	94	149	2.45%	$3.65	63%	5.0%	5.5%	5.2%	8.1%	11.4%	26	66	A-	99	2	R	1837
WLK	Westlake Corp	M	6	-6.0%	NR	116	1.23%	$1.43	7%	20.0%	9.0%	24.0%		10.9%	10	17	B+	91	4	O	1986
ROST	Ross Stores	CD	6.5	17.3%	103	106	1.26%	$1.34	28%	8.8%	16.1%	17.9%	22.0%	16.8%	24	1	A	90	3	U	1982
CASS	Cass Info Sys	IT	7	17.3%	53	43.3	2.68%	$1.16	46%	3.6%	10.1%	10.4%	10.0%	5.6%	16	27	A	99	3	R	1906
CAT	Caterpillar	I	7	2.7%	90	229	2.10%	$4.80	34%	8.1%	7.0%	13.0%	10.0%	12.9%	16	28	A	93	2	O	1925
CMI	Cummins	I	7	16.5%	174	239	2.63%	$6.28	36%	8.3%	7.1%	15.5%	17.0%	11.2%	21	16	B+	98	3	O	1919
FAST	Fastenal	I	7	-9.2%	39	54	2.59%	$1.40	65%	11.0%	13.5%	13.3%	30.0%	18.1%	25	23	A+	81	2	R	1967
GPC	Genuine Parts	CD	7	32.8%	104	167	2.28%	$3.80	43%	9.8%	4.4%	6.1%	5.5%	14.1%	21	65	A-	72	2	O	1925
KMB	Kimberly Clark	CS	7	9.0%	118	134	3.52%	$4.72	82%	1.8%	4.4%	5.0%	7.6%	8.7%	23	49	B+	88	3	U	1872
MSFT	Microsoft	IT	7	-6.2%	165	288	0.94%	$2.72	29%	9.7%	10.0%	12.7%		27.5%	25	12	A-	99	4	R	1975
NKE	Nike	CD	7	-8.9%	72	123	1.11%	$1.36	36%	11.0%	11.2%	13.1%	16.0%	16.8%	34	20	A-	99	3	U	1964
UPS	UPS	I	7	-9.5%	NR	194	3.34%	$6.48	47%	49.0%	6.0%	7.0%	9.0%	11.9%	14	12	A	69	3	O	1907
MRK	Merck & Co	HC	7.5	29.7%	74	106	2.75%	$2.92	37%	5.8%	7.4%	5.4%	3.0%	14.0%	15	10	B+	99	2	R	1891
CAH	Cardinal Health	HC	8	33.2%	76	75.5	2.62%	$1.98	39%	1.0%	1.7%	8.4%	16.0%	9.5%	14	30	B+	74	2	O	1971

Ticker Symbol	Company	Sector	52w	One year return	IQT Under Value Price	Cur Price	Dividend Yield	Dividend	Payout Ratio	Cur Div GR	5Y ADGR	10Y ADGR	20Y ADGR	Annual %return 2013 to 2023	P/E <20	Years of Div incr	S&P	Div Safe	MS value 5 is best	SSD VR	Since
CSCO	Cisco	IT	8	-6.7%	NR	52.3	2.98%	$1.56	44%	2.7%	8.3%	13.4%		12.4%	13	11	A-	91	4	R	1984
IPG	Interpublic	C	8	5.1%	19	37.2	3.33%	$1.24	42%	6.9%	12.0%	16.6%	5.0%	14.8%	13	9	A-	70	3	O	1930
ITW	Illinois Tool Works	I	8	16.3%	142	243	2.16%	$5.24	55%	7.4%	14.7%	13.0%	13.3%	16.2%	23	50	A-	81	2	R	1912
LMT	Lockheed Martin	I	8	7.1%	293	473	2.54%	$12.00	42%	7.1%	9.4%	12.6%	17.0%	21.2%	18	19	A	84	3	R	1995
PEP	PepsiCo	CS	8	8.9%	123	182	2.53%	$4.60	67%	10.0%	7.5%	7.7%	11.0%	13.5%	25	49	B+	93	3	R	1898
PH	Parker-Hannifn	I	8	18.5%	190	336	1.58%	$5.32	26%	29.0%	11.4%	11.1%	12.0%	14.7%	15	66	A-	94	3	O	1917
SBUX	Starbucks	CS	8	14.5%	NR	105	2.02%	$2.12	68%	8.2%	16.9%	20.9%		16.0%	29	12	A-	67	3	R	1971
SNA	Snap-on Co	I	8	20.2%	196	247	2.62%	$6.48	35%	14.0%	15%	14.7%	9.0%	13.8%	14	12	A+	99	2	R	1920
WSO	Watsco	I	8	4.4%	196	318	3.08%	$9.80	60%	11.0%	16.2%	13.1%	24.0%	15.7%	18	8	A+	55	1	R	1945
PPG	PPG Industries	M	8.5	1.9%	99	134	1.85%	$2.48	40%	5.1%	8.0%	7.2%	5.0%	8.3%	19	50	A-	93	2	R	1883
TJX	TJX Co	CD	8.5	29.4%	54	78.4	1.70%	$1.33	37%	13.0%	16.0%	19.2%	21.0%	15.0%	23	1	A-	80	2	R	1987
TTC	Toro Co	I	8.5	30.0%	76	111	1.23%	$1.36	27%	13.0%	11.4%	18.5%	20.0%	19.2%	23	13	A+	84	2	R	1914
AOS	A. O. Smith	I	9	8.2%	32	69.2	1.73%	$1.20	36%	7.1%	17.6%	21.6%	17.1%	15.2%	18	28	A	99	3	R	1874
CLX	Clorox	CS	9	13.8%	118	158	2.99%	$4.72	142%	1.7%	8.0%	6.8%	9.0%	9.4%	31	45	A+	75	4	U	1913
LECO	Lincoln Electric	I	9	22.7%	88	169	1.51%	$2.56	28%	14.0%	9.8%	12.7%	10.6%	14.4%	17	28	B+	98	3	O	1895
ROK	Rockwell Auto	I	9	4.8%	118	293	1.61%	$4.72	46%	5.4%	8.1%	9.9%	10.0%	14.1%	24	13	A-	70	3	O	1903
AVGO	Broadcom	IT	9.5	1.9%	NR	642	2.87%	$18.40	44%	12.0%	29.0%	39.0%		36.1%	14	12	3B-	67	3	O	1961
MCD	McDonalds	CD	9.5	13.1%	169	280	2.17%	$6.08	56%	10.0%	7.8%	7.6%	17.0%	14.3%	26	45	B+	77	2	R	1940
OMC	Omnicom	C	9.5	11.2%	78	94.3	2.97%	$2.80	40%	0.0%	5.5%	10.8%	10.0%	7.1%	12	1	A+	70	3	O	1986
RS	Reliance Steel	M	9.5	40.0%	113	257	1.56%	$4.00	12%	27.0%	10.8%	19.1%	17.0%	15.0%	10	11	A-	73	3	O	1939
GGG	Graco Inc	I	10	4.7%	51	73	1.29%	$0.94	33%	12.0%	11.3%	10.4%	14.0%	16.0%	25	29	A	99	3	U	1926
NJR	New Jersey Resource	U	10	16.0%	45	53.2	2.93%	$1.56	51%	7.6%	7%	6.5%	7.0%	13.5%	20	27	A	74	2	R	1981
TXN	Texas Instruments	IT	10	1.4%	146	186	2.67%	$4.96	48%	7.8%	20.8%	22.4%	22.0%	21.1%	21	18	A+	90	3	U	1930

Ace List column descriptions

Ticker Symbol: Remember this list is informational, showing data as of April 3, 2023, and it is not a prescriptive recommendation for your investments. Invest at your own risk.

Company: The company's name.

Sector: Which sector the company is categorized in:

- BS: Business Services

- D: Consumer Discretionary

- CS: Consumer Staples

- E: Energy

- F: Financials

- HC: Healthcare

- I: Industrials

- IT: Information Technology

- M: Materials

- RE: Real Estate

- U: Utilities

- C: Communications

52W: This is the 52-week price range of the stock. The stock list is arranged so the stocks that are at their lowest price are on the top of the list and are possibly good buys. Zero (0) represents the lowest price the stock has reached within the last 52 weeks. Ten (10) represents the 52-week high. This is the highest price the stock has reached within the last 52 weeks. A #1 represents the 10% off the low price. Below are examples of a 1; 2.5; 5; and 9.

52-Week Range	$70.24 ▼	$196.52	52-Week Range	$107.07 ▼	$181.78
52-Week Range	$59.08 ▼	$80.95	52-Week Range	$53.69 ▼	$81.17

Buying stocks when they are undervalued is one of the most important criteria in stock selection. It is always better to buy stocks when they are at their lowest price. Consider buying stocks that are in the 0 to 3 range of their 52-week low/high range.

YTD Return: What was the year-to-date return as of 3 April, 2023?

IQT Un Val Price: This is the stock price at which the IQT Newsletter considers the company's stock to be undervalued (more about IQT in the next chapter).

Cur Price: This is the current stock price (as of 3 April, 2023).

Dividend Yield: The current yield as a percentage (dividend/price x 100).

Dividend: The current annual cash dividend per share.

Payout Ratio: This is the percentage of company's earnings paid out in the form of a cash dividend. Ideally, we would like the payout to be less than 60%.

Cur Div GR followed by **5Y AGDR, 10Y AGDR** and **20Y AGDR**: This is the current dividend growth rate, followed by the average dividend growth rate for each of the specified time periods. Dividend growth is the most important ingredient in successful dividend investing over time.

Stock Total Return and Dividend Reinvestment (DRIP) average for 10 years from 1 January 2013 until 1 February 2023. https://dqydj.com/stock-return-calculator/

PE<20: This is the price-to-earnings ratio (price/earnings).

Years of Div Incr: The number of consecutive years that dividends have increased for the company.

S&P: The S&P Earnings and Dividend Quality Ranking. This is a widely recognized benchmark of corporate quality. Rankings in the A- or higher range are preferable, as they represent a history of high earnings and dividend quality.

Div Safe: Dividend safety rating from Simply Safe Dividends. 90% of the companies on this list are in the safe or very safe category.

- 81 to 100: very safe

- 61 to 80: safe

- 40 to 60: borderline safe

- 21 to 40 unsafe

- 0 to 20 very unsafe

- Simply Safe Dividends safety ratings: https://www.simplysafedividends.com/dividend-safety-scores

Morningstar valuation rating—a 2 Rating means the stock is overvalued, a 3 rating means it's trading within a range we consider fairly valued, a 4 rating means it's undervalued, and a 5 rating means it's significantly undervalued.

SSD VR: Simply Safe Dividends Value Rating:

- U: undervalued

- R: reasonably priced

- O: overvalued

Since: The year the company was founded.

Over 90% of the stocks in the Ace List are in the IQT newsletter, which is discussed in the next chapter. Focus on those that are in the undervalued section of the newsletter. You may want to put others that you are interested in on a watch list until they reached the recommended undervalued price in the IQT newsletter. The undervalued section in the current IQT newsletter will be your best guide to determine which stocks are best to buy now.

Guidelines for choosing dividend stocks

Own companies that you can understand how they operate. The simpler it is, the better. Take the example of McDonald's. They make and sell fast food. Simple!

The company's payout ratio should be less than 60%. For mature companies, an ideal ratio would between 15% and 60% of their total earnings. As an income investor, high payout ratios are good for you, since it means more income. However, you don't want it to be so high that it begins affecting the company's long-term health. The problem with high (greater than 75%) payout ratios is that they may be unsustainable in downturns. Also eliminate any negative payout ratios from your list. Ideally, utilities should be below 75% and REITs or limited partnerships (MLPs) should be below 90%.

A company with a payout ratio of 100% or more should be avoided. Unless earnings increase, the dividend will eventually be cut. It may still be worth investing into a company with a payout ratio of more than 100% if it has been paying increasing dividends consistently for many years, as long as the payout ratio drops over time. Strong dividend companies such as Clorox (CLX) can have high payout ratios, but it can change from month to month.

The average payout ratio for a Dividend King stock (a company with a record of raising annual dividend payout amounts for at least 50 consecutive years) is 54%. The only exception to this rule is REITs (real estate investment trusts), which are mandated to pay out 90% of their net income, so their yields will naturally be higher.

Buy stocks that are close to their 52-week low point. For the stock past 52-weeks range, use the research tools on your Schwab online account. It is best to focus on companies that are trading somewhere near a 52-week low, indicating that they are undervalued. In the list above, look at stocks on the 52w column that are 0 to 3. Do not buy a stock that is any closer to its high point above 60% (6 in the column). For anything higher, wait for the stock prices to drop by putting in "good until cancelled" limit buy orders.

Diversification is an important part of this investment philosophy, as it spreads your risk over many different investment sectors to help reduce individual portfolio losses. Ideally, you would like your portfolio to spread over 6 to 8 sectors. Initially you may not want to invest more than 5% of your money in any one company.

Over time these percentages will change, as some companies will do better than others. Some companies will significantly increase in value and may make up 15% to 20% of your portfolio. Do not sell or take profits from these high growth stocks. Use the dividends from the high growth stocks to buy other undervalued dividend companies you own. Remember Warren Buffett's coffee can approach to investing. You keep all the companies that continued to pay and increase dividends and don't sell them. Don't make investing complicated. You don't need a lot of companies to become successful.

Never invest all your money in a single venture. This is a gigantic rookie mistake and can cause a financial disaster that takes years to recover from. Most seasoned investors have an extremely diversified portfolio, comprising many different market sectors of dividend paying blue-chip stock investments. Investment in a variety of stocks will lead you to have different financial goals and expectations from each of them. Besides keeping you from a financial disaster, a diversified portfolio of 15 to 25 stocks will expand your options to grow your wealth. So, if you find two appealing companies you'd like to invest in, don't pick one. Invest in both.

Invest in companies with low debt: This is not a major factor with great companies, but I would rather own a company with a debt to equity of 0 (no debt). Companies with low or no debt can more easily resist or outlast market downturns. We like to see debt of 50% or less of the company's total market capitalization. Debt to equity ratio can range from 0 to 3.0 (300%) or even higher. From an income investor's perspective, stability is all important.

Steady revenue and earnings growth: When looking for the best dividend stocks to own for the long term, prioritize stability in the companies you consider. Erratic revenue (up one year, down the next) and all-over-the-board earnings can be signs of trouble.

Durable competitive advantages: This is perhaps the most important feature to look for. A durable competitive advantage (wide moat) can come in several forms, such as a proprietary technology, high barriers to entry, high customer switching costs, or a powerful brand name like McDonald's and Coca-Cola, just to name a few. Check out the Morningstar Moat ratings.

The price-to-earnings (P/E) ratio is less than 20. The market average P/E is somewhere around 15. If the ratio exceeds 20, then it means that the stock is overpriced. The lower the P/E ratio, the better, but be cautious of P/E below 10. The price-to-earnings ratio is a simple metric you could use to find out whether the stock you are interested in is trading at a fair price or is overvalued and expensive. Go to Yahoo Finance to find out the P/E ratio for any stock.

If you think there will be a recession, be more cautious about bank stocks that cut their dividend in the last recession of 2008 to 2009. Banks usually pay a high dividend yield and have good dividend growth, but during the recession of 2008 to 2009, they had a significant drop in price and cut or almost eliminated dividends.

US Bancorp (USB) dropped from $37 to $9 per share over a six-month period between September 2008 and March 2009. They cut their dividend in March 2009 from $1.70 to only $0.20 per share. It took 11 years to get back to $1.70 per share dividend yield. During the COVID-19 bear market, USB shares dropped from $60 to $30 a share, but they did not cut dividends. Many of these bank stocks can drop 50% to 80% over a year's time. There is very little warning because the dividends are not cut until the stock price hits bottom.

At the bottom of a recession or deep bear market might be a good time to buy dividend paying bank stocks if the dividend yield is high enough. USB moved from $30 to more than $60 a share in a year and a half from its March 2020 low. But if you feel a recession is coming, it may be a good idea to focus on other sectors for your investments.

The US Treasury yield curve has been a reliable predictor of recessions in the world's largest economy. Long-dated debt, such as 10-year and 30-year government bonds, usually have higher yields than two and five-year bonds as investors are compensated for keeping their money locked up for longer. As of March 2022, short-term bonds are now higher than long-term bonds.

This rare inversion has become one of investors' most trusted signals of a recession. The flipping of two-year and 10-year Treasury yields has been followed by a U.S. recession every time it has happened in the last 50 years. The recession typically follows within 18 months. There are no bank stocks that cut dividends during the 2008–2009 recessions in the Ace list of stocks. Two banks that increased or maintained their dividends during the last recession were First of Long Island Corporation (FLIC) and Bank OZK (OZK).

Beta (β) is the easiest way to measure the volatility of a stock. Beta is a measure of volatility, and it's often substituted as a measure of risk. I'd like to reiterate that volatility does not equal risk. It equals risk only for someone looking for steady income without significant drawdowns. The overall market index is pegged with a value of one. A beta value greater than one indicates a stock that is more volatile than the market average. A beta value that is less than one indicates a stock that is less volatile than the market. If steady income without a massive upside is your main goal, low beta stocks are the kind you should prioritize owning. Your goals should be to earn decent gains (not the highest) with as much stability as possible. To demonstrate this, here are some five-year Beta values for some popular companies:

- Coke (KO): 0.67

- IBM: 1.09

- McDonald's (MCD): 0.6

"When we own portions of outstanding businesses with outstanding managements, our favorite holding period is forever."
—WARREN BUFFETT—

Biggest dividend investing mistakes

1. Chasing high dividend yield.

2. Putting all your money into a few stocks and sectors.

3. Not doing your research on the company.

4. Losing patience with this type of investment. You plan to keep these stocks forever unless dividends are cut.

5. Not reinvesting your dividends.

6. Not routinely adding more money from your bank into your investment account each month to invest in these dividend stocks.

7. Holding your money in cash, waiting for the best time to buy. When you have money in your account, buy the best undervalued stock at that time, and then you will be getting a constant source of income from that money.

8. Obsessing over the market and listening to financial news. Look at your account and the market only when you have money available to buy more stocks.

9. Not buying more companies during market corrections of 10% to 30% drop in the market.

◆   ◆   ◆

The IQT Newsletter

T he *Investment Quality Trends (IQT) newsletter* will show you how to buy great dividend blue-chip companies with good dividend yields, undervalued, and at the best price.

I have no connection with the IQT newsletter, other than I like and use their services. This newsletter does all the homework for you to determine which are the best dividend-paying stocks in the market. Of the 292 companies that are in the newsletter, they determine which ones are undervalued, allowing you to buy these companies at good prices and high dividend yields.

In 1966, Geraldine Weiss, the Grand Dame of Dividends, co-founded the *Investment Quality Trends* (IQT) newsletter. She introduced the dividend-yield approach, which measures and selects stocks that are great value and great buys. She described the use of her newsletter in her 1988 book with Janet Lowe *Dividends Don't Lie*. In 2002, she passed the torch to Kelley Wright, who continues as editor and publisher of *Investment Quality Trends*.

He followed up with an updated-version 2010 book, *Dividends Still Don't Lie*. The companies listed in the IQT newsletter have long dividend histories and well-etched profiles of undervalue and overvalue. The newsletter includes many of the Dividend Aristocrats. Most of them carry an S&P Quality Rank of A+, A, or A-. They are, in fact, true blue-chips.

Dividends are the most reliable measure of value in the stock market. Earnings are figures on the balance sheet that can be manipulated for income tax purposes. Dividends are real money, and, once paid, it is gone forever from the company. When a company increases its dividend, you don't have to read a balance sheet to know that the company has made profitable progress. In short, **Dividends Don't Lie.**

Kelley Wright says investing is a business and should be treated as such. If you want to gamble, go to Las Vegas. If you have personal issues that need to be worked out, get a therapist. If you want to be successful in the stock market, learn how to identify quality businesses that offer historic value, and then make the most efficient use of your resources.

After 56 years, *Investment Quality Trends* continues to help investors master the stock market by helping them select high-quality, dividend-paying, blue-chip stocks. A blue-chip stock is a nationally recognized, well-established, and financially sound company. These companies generally sell high-quality, widely accepted products and services. Blue-chip stocks are known to weather downturns and operate profitably in the face of adverse economic conditions, which help to contribute to their long record of stable and reliable growth.

The most important pieces of the puzzle are identifying high-quality companies with long track records of managerial competence and financial achievement that are bought when they offer excellent internal cash flow and historical good value. This is what Warren Buffett does in determining which stocks he buys. You want great companies, which are well managed, and to buy them at a good value.

The *IQT* Newsletter does all the research for you

IQT confines their investment selections to time-tested, high-quality, blue-chip stocks with long histories of unbroken dividend payouts and attractive records of earnings and dividend growth. The companies should have reasonably low levels of debt. The stocks should have relatively low price-to-earnings ratios. The newsletter shows you when stocks are undervalued and the maximum price you should pay per share.

According to their method, a stock will achieve the designation of select blue-chip after it has met at least 5 of the 6 following qualifications and may remain with 4 criteria:

* Dividend increases 5 times in the last 12 years

* S&P Quality Ranking in the "A" category

* At least 5,000,000 shares outstanding

- At least 80 institutional investors

- At least 25 years of uninterrupted dividends

- Earnings improved in at least 7 of the last 12 years

Historically, by looking at the dividend yield and the company's long term dividend yield pattern, you can determine when these stocks are undervalued or overvalued. This also helps you determine the price you should pay for those stocks. The undervalued stocks give a high yield return, offering the least downside risk and the greatest upside potential.

From *IQT*'s list of undervalued stocks, you want to select 15 to 25 stocks that are diversified across 5 to 7 of the 11 different industrial sectors. Diversification in strong, blue-chip companies will significantly reduce your risk. You will select your stocks from the **undervalued area** of the newsletter, giving you greater potential for profit of the stock and high dividend yield. The profit will be recognized on the sell when the stock reaches overvalued. Everything in between is just distraction and noise.

These blue-chip stocks are undervalued when the dividend percentage yield is at their historical high, such as 2.5% to 6.5% with an average of 3.5%. This is the premise and basis of the *IQT* newsletter. These undervalued blue-chip stocks are ideal for investors that want a consistent high interest rate of income. These are companies that increase their dividends each year. Some increase them by more than 10%, resulting in doubling return in 7 years, and quadrupling your return in 14 years. Stocks are considered overvalued when the stock price rises high enough that the dividend yield becomes historically low between 0.3% and 2%, with an average of around 1%.

The only critique is that some stocks remain in the undervalued area for a significant amount of time before they begin to demonstrate price appreciation. For the investors with a long-term investment time-horizon, this is not an issue, as they are getting paid to wait from consistent dividend payments and dividend income increases.

There are multifaceted explanations and reasons for why a stock may remain in the undervalued area for an extended period. Sometimes these companies fall out of favor with Wall Street, but we need to focus on their excellent current value in terms of their dividend yield and dividend-income growth.

When markets are at all-time highs, it may take you a year to get your list filled. You need to be patient and pay no more than *IQT*'s undervalued number for those stocks off the list. But there are always corrections, as we saw in March 2020, when there was a 32% drop in the S&P 500.

Our most recent correction, in 2022, saw the S&P 500 drop down to a negative -27.5%. From January 3, 2022, until November 2022, the S&P 500 was down -16%. During the same timeframe, my dividend portfolio from my Ace List grew 12% . . . a difference of 28%. During times like this, you could have completely filled your wish list of undervalued, blue-chip stocks in a few days.

IQT-recommended price for undervalued stocks

The *IQT* newsletter will recommend what to pay for stocks when they drop to the under-valued category. When purchasing these stocks undervalued, they have the potential to even double in price over the next few years. Be ready to find money and take advantage of these great opportunities.

Let us examine how and why dividends create value in the stock market. When the price of a stock declines far enough to produce a high dividend yield, institutional investors and value-minded investors who seek income begin to buy. The further the price falls, the higher the yield becomes, and the more investors are drawn to the stock. Eventually the stock becomes irresistibly undervalued, and dividend yields are very high, buyers outnumber sellers, the decline is reversed, and the stock begins to rise.

As the price per share of the stock rises higher, the dividend yield becomes lower, and fewer investors are attracted to the stock. Eventually the price becomes so high, and the dividend yield is so low, sellers outnumber buyers, and the price of the stock begins to decline. Those investors who purchased the stock at lower levels are inclined to sell and take their profits.

My recommendation is that you never sell great companies. Remember, as their prices increase, your dividend yield increases for the shares you bought. The only time you sell these companies is when their dividends are cut or they stop paying dividends.

It is very rare that any companies on the *IQT* newsletter will cut dividends. A few exceptions have been banks during the last recession, and also Boeing and Disney in the

2020 COVID market drop. When this happened, the *IQT* newsletter let you know that these companies cut their dividends.

Dividend success example

My friend, a dentist (we will call him DDS), introduced me to the *IQT* newsletter to help me buy great dividend paying companies when they are undervalued and what price to pay. In 2000, DDS started investing in dividend paying stocks to prepare for his early retirement. DDS spent a lot of time researching the thousands of dividends paying stocks in the market. In 2007, he was introduced to the *IQT* newsletter by a retired dentist and longtime user of the newsletter. He started to exclusively use only the *IQT* newsletter for all his stock selection from the undervalued list. It was simple to use, because they did all the research for him. He just enjoyed his life and never worried about what was happening in the market.

DDS retired debt-free at age 50 in 2008, with $1.5 million invested in the market. He was receiving more than $60,000 that year in dividends. The next year, just after he retired, his portfolio dropped 44% during the great recession. Surprisingly, his dividends increased in 2009 to $80,000. This was because he never sold his stocks; he continued to buy more undervalued blue-chip stocks on sale, using the proceeds from his dividends. Also, when prices drop, many great companies increase their dividends to keep their investors.

Over the next 13 years, he lived on 85% of the dividends and reinvested the other 15% of the dividends back into his portfolio. As of December 2022, his portfolio was worth $10 million, and his annual dividend payout is now more than $360,000. This is an average annual dividend growth return of 12.8% since 2009. Many of the companies listed in this book have even greater dividend growth. That is the power of continued increasing dividend growth!!!

Over the past 13 years of investing in dividends stocks, DDS will receive an incredible 11.12% return on his dividends this year on his original cost basis of $3,046,000. His overall average annual return in his portfolio using the *IQT* newsletter from 2009 to 2022 was 19.4%, which was 4% higher than the S&P 500 average annual return of 15.3%, without dividend reinvestment.

DDS loves this approach to investing because he does not need to do any research. He spends only about an hour a month reading the *IQT* newsletter and puts in a limit or market buy order for a selected stock if the price is below the recommended price listed in the "undervalued" section of the newsletter. He usually puts in "good until canceled" limit orders one or two points below the newsletter's recommendation for the undervalued stock price. Then, over the next 60 days, he will wait to see if his order is accepted.

He then sits back, relaxes, receives his dividends, and never worries about money or the ups and downs of the market. This once-a-month approach is like dollar cost averaging, protecting you against your emotions and large swings in the market. He and his wife both have their own Schwab accounts and invest each month. She also does her own investments using the IQT newsletter. He now has a new updated airplane, and they just bought a new home and paid cash.

My friend told me that in the past, like most investors, he had focused on the price of the stock. He has now realized that was the wrong number, as stock prices continually fluctuate up and down and are not that important to a long-term investor. DDS now knows the most important numbers to focus on are the dividend growth, total annual stock return, and the passive income returns he gets every month.

- To see how much income from your dividends you have received and will be receiving over the next 12 months in your Schwab account, click "investment income" on the upper banner of your account.

The Buffett mindset

For those investors who are still working, you can reinvest 100% of your dividends *plus* invest added money each month, growing your dividend portfolio exponentially. Warren Buffett understands this concept well. His company Berkshire Hathaway does not pay dividends to their investors but reinvests all the dividends received from the companies under the umbrella of Berkshire Hathaway. Of the 48 securities within Berkshire Hathaway's holdings, 34 companies pay a regular dividend. In 2021, Buffett's Berkshire Hathaway annually receives $6.07 billion in dividends.

Warren Buffett, like DDS, rarely worries about the ups and downs in the market, knowing that the main goal is the returns on dividends. He plans to keep these companies forever and receive the continual cash flow of dividends. In fact, he is hoping for a down market to buy great companies that have become undervalued.

Buffett understands that, eventually, those companies that he owns under the umbrella of Berkshire Hathaway will continue to go up in time. He once said: "I never attempt to make money on the stock market. I buy on the assumption that they could close the market the next day and not reopen it for five years." It would not make a difference to long-term investors because they are in for the dividend passive income. If you want to know which blue-chip companies that Warren Buffett invests in, go to his annual report, and see how many Dividend Aristocrats he owns.

- ◆ Berkshire Hathaway annual reports:
  http://www.berkshirehathaway.com/letters/letters.html

Reinvesting dividends

The fastest way to grow your wealth is to reinvest your dividends into undervalued blue-chip companies. If the stock becomes overvalued, use the dividends from that stock to buy more undervalued companies. All dividends are put into your Schwab cash account. Continue to add more cash to your Schwab account along with the dividend cash. Each month you will go through the *IQT* newsletter and use that cash to buy more undervalued blue-chip stocks.

Make sure that you set aside 15% to 20% to pay taxes on your dividend income in your individual account if it is not tax-deferred. There will be no tax on your retirement tax-deferred accounts.

When the stock rises in price to the overvalued area, you may consider selling them and reinvesting the money in more undervalued blue-chip stocks. I would probably only do this if the stocks were in a tax-deferred account such as an IRA, Roth IRA, or a 401K plan. In these accounts, you do not have to pay the capital gains tax on the sale of the stock. I would recommend not selling stocks in a taxable account even if they are overvalued but using their dividends to invest in more undervalued companies.

The advantages of buying dividend paying stocks in the *IQT* list of great blue-chip companies are listed below.

1. These companies have already been vetted, and you have at your fingertips the most important data to help you make your decision.

2. Companies that pay consistent dividends (over 25 years plus) indicate they are solid companies.

3. You get a reliable dividend income even in down markets.

4. These companies have long-term potential, which keeps you in the stock longer.

5. Upside potential is higher because you bought these companies when they were undervalued.

6. The dividend yield of these undervalued companies is higher than bonds and the S&P 500 index dividends.

7. The market's long-term returns come mostly from dividends. Dividends account for about 75% of the S&P 500 Index's long-term returns.

8. These blue-chip companies become your consistent source of retirement income.

9. You never worry about the ups and downs of the market, and you easily fall asleep each night.

Start investing NOW

- Buy those selected undervalued stocks that you like on the Dr. Aces Freedom Fund list, focusing on the undervalued stocks. Initially, start slow, with small amounts, to familiarize yourself with the process and get comfortable buying these stocks.

- Do your research using the *IQT* newsletter, simplysafedividends.com, and the research section of your Schwab account..

- Investing each month using your available cash is like dollar cost averaging in the market, which eventually will give you a great return.

- Buy stocks in 5 to 7 sectors and 15 to 25 stocks to reduce your risk and worry about individual portfolio losses. Try not to have any more than 5% of your money in any one company.

- Read the Appendix: Summary Guide to Dividend Growth Investing for guidelines to select your stocks.

- Sit back and relax.

- You need to look at your portfolio only once a month when you have added money into your account to buy more stocks. Other than that, you should not be even thinking about your portfolio or what the market is doing.

Whatever you decide to do, **the most important thing is to just get started**. You don't have to wait for a big downturn in the market. The sooner you start investing in dividend stocks, the sooner you will start building wealth and creating passive income. Time is the greatest advantage that you can have in the stock market. If you combine compounding with time, you have the perfect recipe for building wealth.

◆ ◆ ◆

Final Thoughts

he greatest destroyers of investment wealth are expenses (advisor fees, brokerage commissions), taxes, inflation, misinformation, and not getting started to invest.

Misinformation

Over the past 60 years, we have been imprinted through our culture with financial myths, half-truths, and lies by those who want to take our discretionary income and keep us poor. Once we look closely at the myths, we realize how these lies keep us from reaching true personal and financial freedom.

One such myth perpetuated by banks, financial advisors, accountants, and Wall Street is that debt is normal and that you would make more money by investing with them instead of paying off your house early. They also say that you will lose the tax benefit of writing off your mortgage interest. In most cases, this is not true, but they are the key reasons people do not pay off their home and stay in debt. The truth is that you can earn more than 200% return on your money by paying off the home early.

Pay off debt quickly while you are learning the dividend investment strategy. Paying off debt always gives you your greatest and safest return of any investment. Paying off that gives you a guaranteed interest rate of more than 100%, risk-free. Set up an automatic payment each month toward the principal of your next debt in your debt-elimination payments.

- Go to www.doctorace.com to check out all the myths that keep us poor. You will find videos and audios on debt elimination, plus a free downloadable copy of my books.

Eliminate taxes and place your money in a safe, no-risk environment

The money you have for investment can be put into the Schwab money-market account (SWVXX) while you're waiting to buy dividend paying stocks. This fund is now paying over 4% annual interest. These are not FDIC-insured, but they are SIPC-insured up to $500,000. This fund is available for individual retirement and investment accounts. Your money can be accessed anytime for an emergency or to invest in the market when companies are on sale.

You can now put limit orders on those companies that are on your watch list. Once the order is executed, make sure that you sell enough money from your money market account to cover the purchase of the stock.

If you are an investor with a shorter-term investment time-horizon, emotionally cannot tolerate swings in the market, or lack the discipline and patience required to hold companies' long-term, then CDs, bonds and U.S. Treasuries were recommended in the past. The idea of creating a nest egg and living off the interest income from these investments can vary from year to year and range from 0.1% up to 4% we are now receiving. Dividend growth investing is a much more predictable way to invest your money while receiving great returns.

The best long-term option as described in this book are undervalued dividend paying blue-chip stocks. You could easily live off the dividends and never, ever have to touch or sell the stocks.

Taxes are the biggest destroyer of individual wealth. What are the best types of investments to minimize the amount of taxes you pay? These are: paying off debt, Roth IRA, 529 plans, health savings accounts (HSAs), and qualified dividend-paying blue-chip stocks. Stop funding the standard tax-deferred investments in your 401K, and focus more on the Roth portion of your 401K.

If you have a 401K plan at your office, maximize the Roth portion of that plan. The new 2023 Secure Act 2.0 has significantly improved the ability to have more money placed in the Roth portion of your 401K. Check with your CPA and your 401K plan administrator to see the real advantages of this act.

Freedom and legacy

When Mohandas Gandhi was asked *What is your message to the world?* he replied: "My life is my message." What is the message you want to teach your children about money and freedom in your life?

One of the greatest gifts you can give your children is to teach them these concepts about getting out of debt, saving money, and investing safely through dividend investing. This is how we leave a legacy for them to become strong, self-sufficient adults.

- To learn the specific steps of getting out of debt, go to Dave Ramsey Financial Peace University: https://www.ramseysolutions.com/ramseyplus/financial-peace.

Set up a Schwab account for each one of your children, and teach them how to invest in dividend stocks. Maximize their Roth IRA benefits each year. Show them how they can buy a few shares of Coke or McDonald's. When they start this habit young, they will learn to love creating passive income for the rest of their life.

There are different strategies using blue-chip dividend paying stocks to reduce or even avoid taxes. You and your spouse can give each child up to $34,000 a year in a Schwab investment account, and all the dividends will be tax free if your child earns less than $40,000 a year. As your children get older and are married, you give up to $60,000 to both children and pass on your legacy through these dividend-paying blue-chip stocks.

Another way to avoid paying taxes on appreciated investments is to donate those investments. Donating appreciated assets dissolves taxation levied on the capital gains. Neither you nor the receiver will have to pay the taxes. Moreover, donations not only make you feel as if you are giving back to the community by contributing your wealth—they also make you feel good about being successful and influential.

By investing in dividend producing blue-chip stocks, you create a constant source of passive income for the rest of your life. During that time, these stocks continue to appreciate because you don't sell them. When you die, assets in a taxable account are passed on to your heirs in the next generation. This transference of assets resets the cost basis to the current value. The assets can then be sold without having to pay any taxes. This results in a huge tax break.

The secret to your financial success through investing is to *Start Now*. Start small to build up your confidence. Follow the steps described, and enjoy the process. Good luck, and have fun.

◆　◆　◆

Appendix:
Summary Guide to
Dividend-Growth Investing

- Go to www.doctorace.com/dividendlinks/ to quickly access links to all the online resources that are referenced in this book.

When to buy

The following criteria are what I use in my own portfolio selection, but everyone should make their own set of guidelines. Investors should tailor their stock selection to meet their own individual needs and goals.

- All companies purchased should be on Dividend Achiever list (10 years of increasing dividends), with the vast majority (85%) having at least a 15-year growth history of dividend increases. This list also includes the Dividend Aristocrats and Dividend Kings.

- Use the Ace List in this book as a starting point for evaluating stock selection for dividend-growth investing. The stocks on the Ace List have been researched and selected to meet the guidelines outlined in this book.

- The key to successful investing is buying companies that pay dividends and increase dividends yearly. Buying these companies may increase your return by 2% or more over the average S&P 500 return.

- The best time to buy these companies are when they are undervalued. This is called "value investing," and you look for companies that are trading for less than their intrinsic or book value. Buying stock when they are undervalued increases your dividend yield, safety from loss, and your equity profitability.

- Over time, the market trends upward, and, during these times, there are fewer companies that are undervalued. When the market reacts to bad news, the price of great companies will go down. These are your buying opportunities. You don't need to understand why bear markets occur, but you do need to take advantage of them.

- You must wait patiently for market corrections to fill your bucket list with the 15 to 25 companies that you will keep forever.

- *IQT* newsletter is probably the best source to select great dividend-paying companies that are undervalued. They also provide an undervalued-price guideline for each stock.

- Because we buy only undervalued companies, the stock must be below 50% of their 52-week price range. Ideally, we would like companies that are at their 52-week low, up to 30% low.

- Valuing a business is somewhat amorphous and ephemeral, with no real precise/fixed number. Looking at a consensus of the best resources as described can help the investor come up with their best estimate and then be super conservative around that estimate. Each investor must formulate their own opinions using available resources, rather than trying to find a precise number where none can ever be found. My best research resources are simplysafedividends.com and the research area in my Schwab account.

- There is a great possibility that we will be heading into a recession. This is why I do not buy any stock that cut their dividends in the last 2008 to 2009 recession. This is true with most bank stocks, even those in the *IQT* newsletter that give high dividend yields.

- The main focus should be on dividend-growth rate, total dollar return, and dividend safety, and less upon high dividend yield. Ideally, we want a current dividend-growth rate of at least 3%, a 5-year average dividend-growth rate of 7% or above, and a greater-than 10% 10-year average dividend-growth rate. We would like to see the total annual stock return with dividend reinvested to be above 10% over any time frame.

- When markets are up, it can be more difficult to find companies yielding 3%, a 7% dividend growth rate, and at least 15 years of dividend growth. I am more lenient on the starting yield, but I balance this with either higher dividend growth or more years of dividend growth.

- Ideally have somewhere between 15 and 30 companies spread over different sectors. No sector should be more than 18% of total income. No individual stock should be more than 10% of total income, ideally 5% to 6%. These are just guidelines. Sometimes I have sectors that exceed the 18% rule, usually due to faster-growing dividends. When this happens, I just quit making new purchases in that sector. I never sell my fast-growing companies, and I let the winners ride.

- No more than two companies owned per industry. No purchasing of mining companies or foreign companies. I am not a fan of real estate REITs or MLPs, as they have non-qualified dividends unless they are in an IRA.

- I shy away from energy companies such as Chevron (CVX) and Exxon Mobil (XOM), because price always seems to fluctuate, depending on the cost of oil, and, over time, the equity value and dividend growth increases slowly. When oil prices are significantly down and dividend yield is extremely high, that is the time to purchase these undervalued energy companies. When those companies become overvalued, it would be worth it to sell them and focus on other undervalued dividend companies in a different sector.

My goal is to have a portfolio that grows at 9% annually without reinvesting dividends and 14% annually when reinvesting dividends. This will effectively double my income every five to six years pre-retirement by reinvesting the dividends. Post-retirement, when I am spending the dividends, I expect to double my income every eight years. This growth is assuming I add no additional capital to the portfolio.

When to sell

A dividend-growth investor purchases a stock with the intent to hold it forever. An investor should personally research a company, understand the story, and expect the company to be around for a long, long time. Selling a company like this should not be taken lightly. Sell only when the dividend is cut, when the dividend has not been increased in a year without an excuse, or when the story has changed. I do not own DOW which has not increased its dividends in three years.

I would also sell when the company is being acquired. When a company announces that it's being bought, the stock will jump in price. It will likely not make it to the planned buyout price, but it will be within a few cents. I usually sell before the buyout. I will take the instant stock-price jump rather than wait and see if it happened. I would have liked to at least have held the stock for one year from my original purchase to take advantage of the tax benefits of long-term capital gains. This is not as important when it is in a tax-deferred account such as an IRA.

Some investors sell a great company when it becomes overvalued. I choose to keep these companies forever and not sell them, especially when my yield on cost is more than 6% and growing. These companies can grow even more. I would use the dividends from these company to reinvest in other undervalued companies of my choice.

Jesse Blair, in his excellent book *The No-Nonsense Guide to Dividend Growth*, states that "Long-term dividend-growth investing discourages lots of trading. A portfolio is like a bar of soap. The more you handle it, the smaller it gets. Studies show that investors who trade often have the worst returns."

That's good advice, but also remember the most important rule in dividend investing: **Sell on a dividend cut**.

◆　◆　◆

CPSIA information can be obtained
at www.ICGtesting.com
Printed in the USA
LVHW060035200723
752910LV00013B/898